Weather and Climate Inventory
National Park Service
Northern Great Plains Network

Natural Resource Technical Report NPS/NGPN/NRTR—2007/039
WRCC Report 2007-14

Christopher A. Davey, Kelly T. Redmond, and David B. Simeral
Western Regional Climate Center
Desert Research Institute
2215 Raggio Parkway
Reno, Nevada 89512-1095

May 2007

U.S. Department of the Interior
National Park Service
Natural Resource Program Center
Fort Collins, Colorado

The Natural Resource Publication series addresses natural resource topics that are of interest and applicability to a broad readership in the National Park Service and to others in the management of natural resources, including the scientific community, the public, and the National Park Service conservation and environmental constituencies. Manuscripts are peer-reviewed to ensure that the information is scientifically credible, technically accurate, appropriately written for the intended audience, and designed and published in a professional manner.

The Natural Resources Technical Reports series is used to disseminate the peer-reviewed results of scientific studies in the physical, biological, and social sciences for both the advancement of science and the achievement of the National Park Service mission. The reports provide contributors with a forum for displaying comprehensive data that are often deleted from journals because of page limitations. Current examples of such reports include the results of research that address natural resource management issues; natural resource inventory and monitoring activities; resource assessment reports; scientific literature reviews; and peer-reviewed proceedings of technical workshops, conferences, or symposia.

Views and conclusions in this report are those of the authors and do not necessarily reflect policies of the National Park Service. Mention of trade names or commercial products does not constitute endorsement or recommendation for use by the National Park Service.

Printed copies of reports in these series may be produced in a limited quantity and they are only available as long as the supply lasts. This report is also available from the Natural Resource Publications Management website (http://www.nature.nps.gov/publications/NRPM) on the Internet or by sending a request to the address on the back cover.

Please cite this publication as follows:

Davey, C. A., K. T. Redmond, and D. B. Simeral. 2007. Weather and Climate Inventory, National Park Service, Northern Great Plains Network. Natural Resource Technical Report NPS/NGPN/NRTR—2007/039. National Park Service, Fort Collins, Colorado.

NPS/NGPN/NRTR—2007/039, May 2007

Contents

Contents (continued)

Figures

Tables

Appendixes

Acronyms

AASC	American Association of State Climatologists
ACIS	Applied Climate Information System
AGFO	Agate Fossil Beds National Monument
ASOS	Automated Surface Observing System
AWDN	Automated Weather Data Network
AWOS	Automated Weather Observing System
BADL	Badlands National Park
BLM	Bureau of Land Management
CASTNet	Clean Air Status and Trends Network
COOP	Cooperative Observer Program
CRN	Climate Reference Network
CWOP	Citizen Weather Observer Program
DETO	Devils Tower National Monument
DFIR	Double-Fence Intercomparison Reference
DST	daylight savings time
ENSO	El Niño Southern Oscillation
EPA	Environmental Protection Agency
FAA	Federal Aviation Administration
FIPS	Federal Information Processing Standards
FOLA	Fort Laramie National Historic Site
FOUS	Fort Union Trading Post National Historic Site
GMT	Greenwich Mean Time
GOES	Geostationary Operational Environmental Satellite
GPMP	NPS Gaseous Pollutant Monitoring Program
GPS	Global Positioning System
GPS-MET	NOAA ground-based GPS meteorology
HPRCC	High Plains Regional Climate Center
I&M	NPS Inventory and Monitoring Program
JECA	Jewel Cave National Monument
KNRI	Knife River Indian Villages National Historic Site
LEO	Low Earth Orbit
LST	local standard time
MDN	Mercury Deposition Network
MNRR	Missouri National Recreational River
MORU	Mount Rushmore National Memorial
MT DOT	Montana Department of Transportation
NADP	National Atmospheric Deposition Program
NASA	National Aeronautics and Space Administration
NCDC	National Climatic Data Center
NetCDF	Network Common Data Form
NGPN	Northern Great Plains Inventory and Monitoring Network
NIOB	Niobrara National Scenic Riverway
NOAA	National Oceanic and Atmospheric Administration
NPS	National Park Service

NRCS	Natural Resources Conservation Service
NRCS-SC	USDA/NRCS snowcourse network
NWS	National Weather Service
PRISM	Parameter Regression on Independent Slopes Model
RAWS	Remote Automated Weather Station
RCC	regional climate center
SAO	Surface Airways Observation network
SCAN	Soil Climate Analysis Network
SCBL	Scotts Bluff National Monument
SOD	Summary Of the Day
Surfrad	Surface Radiation Budget network
SNOTEL	USDA/NRCS Snowfall Telemetry network
THRO	Theodore Roosevelt National Park
UPR	Union Pacific Railroad
USDA	U.S. Department of Agriculture
USGS	U.S. Geological Survey
UTC	Coordinated Universal Time
WBAN	Weather Bureau Army Navy
WICA	Wind Cave National Park
WMO	World Meteorological Organization
WRCC	Western Regional Climate Center
WX4U	Weather For You network
WYDOT	Wyoming Department of Transportation

Executive Summary

Climate is a dominant factor driving the physical and ecologic processes affecting the Northern Great Plains Inventory and Monitoring Network (NGPN). The Northern Great Plains is characterized by extremes in weather ranging from hot dry summers to cold winters with prolonged snow cover. Droughts within the NGPN are important in maintaining grassland communities. High winds often compound the effects of temperature and precipitation on NGPN ecosystems. These large climate variations influence heavily on the composition, structure, and processes of prairie ecosystems. The impact of global climate change may be exacerbated in the Northern Great Plains due to the region's periodic droughts and the large number of habitat specialists. Climate variations do have significant impact on grassland ecosystems. For instance, global warming could increase grassland vegetation and decrease forested and shrubby vegetation. The NGPN network has stressed the importance of site-specific weather and climate monitoring. Climate is one of the 12 basic inventories to be completed for all National Park Service (NPS) Inventory and Monitoring Program (I&M) networks.

This project was initiated to inventory past and present climate monitoring efforts in the NGPN. In this report, we provide the following information:

- Overview of broad-scale climatic factors and zones important to NGPN park units.
- Inventory of weather and climate station locations in and near NGPN park units relevant to the NPS I&M Program.
- Results of an inventory of metadata on each weather station, including affiliations for weather-monitoring networks, types of measurements recorded at these stations, and information about the actual measurements (length of record, etc.).
- Initial evaluation of the adequacy of coverage for existing weather stations and recommendations for improvements in monitoring weather and climate.

Annual precipitation totals in the NGPN region are generally light to moderate, increasing from west to east across the network. Superimposed on this general pattern is a smaller area of higher precipitation which occurs in the Black Hills of South Dakota. Mean annual precipitation ranges from under 400 mm in park units such as FOUS (Fort Union Trading Post National Historic Site), to over 600 mm in eastern portions of MNRR (Missouri National Recreational River). Precipitation in NGPN park units generally peaks in late spring or early summer. Despite being generally light, precipitation in the NGPN is highly variable spatially, especially in the spring and summer, with localized heavy storms. Mean annual temperatures across the NGPN generally increase from north to south, although local topography introduces significant small-scale variations in many NGPN park units. The coldest NGPN park units in North Dakota average below 5°C, while portions of Badlands National Park (BADL) approach 9°C or greater. The mildest park units during the winter months are located in southwest NGPN, closer to downslope wind influences from the Rocky Mountains. Winter temperatures in North Dakota commonly approach -20°C, while summer maximum temperatures are quite warm throughout the NGPN. A significant driver of the interannual climate variations in the NGPN is the El Niño-Southern Oscillation (ENSO), with El Niño conditions (warm ENSO phases) being associated with warmer and drier than normal conditions. While precipitation trends across the NGPN are mixed, temperature trends show warming during the past century.

Through a search of national databases and inquiries to NPS staff, we have identified 30 weather and climate stations within NGPN park units. Theodore Roosevelt National Park (THRO) has the most stations within park boundaries (8). Most of the weather and climate stations we identified had metadata and data records that are sufficiently complete and satisfactory in quality.

We identified numerous long-term climate stations and real-time weather stations near both MNRR and NIOB (Niobrara National Scenic Riverway). However, no real-time stations were identified within the park units themselves. At MNRR, a feasible strategy could be to install an AWDN (Automated Weather Data Network) or RAWS (Remote Automated Weather Station) station at one of the existing COOP (Cooperative Observer Program) sites at Lewis and Clark Lake ("Niobrara" or "Verdel 6 S"). Both MNRR and NIOB have opportunities for setting up local climate transects. For instance, an additional AWDN station at the west end of NIOB would complement the AWDN station "Higgins Ranch" near the east (downstream) end of the park unit, and would allow the park unit to conduct basic climate transect analyses along the Niobrara River.

Both FOUS and KNRI (Knife River Indian Villages National Historic Site) have no near-real-time stations in or immediately near the park units. These park units may want to consider installations of new automated stations (e.g., AWDN or RAWS) to address this need. Both park units must also rely heavily on outside sources of long-term climate information.

No near-real-time weather stations were identified for the north unit and the Elkhorn Ranch unit of THRO. Both the AWDN and RAWS networks could provide suitable installations, focused near the main roadways of the THRO units. The riparian and canyon rim environments of the north unit of THRO could be sampled. New automated weather station installations could also be valuable near the scenic loop in the south unit of THRO. Similar sampling gaps are found at BADL, where most stations are located in northeastern portions of the park unit. Climate conditions in the southwestern portion of BADL remaining largely unsampled. Since the RAWS network already has a large presence in the area, new RAWS stations could be considered.

Many of the NGPN park units in and around the Black Hills have at least one longer climate record and one near-real-time station at the park unit. The one exception to this general pattern is Jewel Cave National Monument (JECA), which has no weather/climate stations within its boundaries and must therefore rely heavily on outside sources of reliable climate records for the area. Climate monitoring activities at JECA will benefit by working with local officials to encourage the continued operation of these weather and climate stations outside of JECA.

Despite significant gaps at "Agate 3 E," this COOP station is an important source for long-term climate data in Agate Fossil Beds National Monument (AGFO). Scotts Bluff National Monument (SCBL) has no long-term climate stations. However, the park unit is located within a few kilometers of valuable climate records in Scottsbluff.

The COOP stations identified for Fort Laramie National Historic Site (FOLA) will provide useful climate records as they continue operating. The closest reliable near-real-time weather stations for FOLA are in Torrington. Automated station installations in FOLA (AWDN or RAWS) could be considered.

Acknowledgements

This work was supported and completed under Task Agreement H8R07010001, with the Great Basin Cooperative Ecosystem Studies Unit. We would like to acknowledge very helpful assistance from various National Park Service personnel associated with the Northern Great Plains Inventory and Monitoring Network. Particular thanks are extended to Dan Licht and Joel Brumm. We also thank John Gross, Margaret Beer, Grant Kelly, Greg McCurdy, and Heather Angeloff for all their help. Seth Gutman with the National Oceanic and Atmospheric Administration Earth Systems Research Laboratory provided valuable input on the GPS-MET station network. Portions of the work were supported by the NOAA Western Regional Climate Center.

1.0. Introduction

Weather and climate are key drivers in ecosystem structure and function. Global- and regional-scale climate variations will have a tremendous impact on natural systems (Chapin et al. 1996; Schlesinger 1997; Jacobson et al. 2000; Bonan 2002). Long-term patterns in temperature and precipitation provide first-order constraints on potential ecosystem structure and function. Secondary constraints are realized from the intensity and duration of individual weather events and, additionally, from seasonality and inter-annual climate variability. These constraints influence the fundamental properties of ecologic systems, such as soil–water relationships, plant–soil processes, and nutrient cycling, as well as disturbance rates and intensity. These properties, in turn, influence the life-history strategies supported by a climatic regime (Neilson 1987; Rodriguez-Iturbe 2000; Licht et al. 2005).

Given the importance of climate, it is one of 12 basic inventories to be completed by the National Park Service (NPS) Inventory and Monitoring Program (I&M) network (I&M 2006). Climate was ranked as the eleventh highest priority Vital Sign in the Northern Great Plains Network, or NGPN (Licht et al. 2005). As primary environmental drivers for the other vital signs, weather and climate patterns present various practical and management consequences and implications for the NPS (Oakley et al. 2003). Most park units observe weather and climate elements as part of their overall mission. The lands under NPS stewardship provide many excellent locations for monitoring climatic conditions.

It is essential that park units within the NGPN have an effective climate-monitoring system in place to track climate changes and to aid in management decisions relating to these changes. The purpose of this report is to determine the current status of weather and climate monitoring within the NGPN (Table 1.1; Figure 1.1). In this report, we provide the following informational elements:

- Overview of broad-scale climatic factors and zones important to NGPN park units.
- Inventory of locations for all weather stations in and near NGPN park units that are relevant to the NPS I&M networks.
- Results of metadata inventory for each station, including weather-monitoring network affiliations, types of recorded measurements, and information about actual measurements (length of record, etc.).
- Initial evaluation of the adequacy of coverage for existing weather stations and recommendations for improvements in monitoring weather and climate.

1.1. Network Terminology
Before proceeding, it is important to stress that this report discusses the idea of "networks" in two different ways. Modifiers are used to distinguish between NPS I&M networks and weather/climate station networks. See Appendix A for a full definition of these terms.

1.1.1. Weather/Climate Station Networks
Most weather and climate measurements are made not from isolated stations but from stations that are part of a network operated in support of a particular mission. The limiting case is a network of one station, where measurements are made by an interested observer or group. Larger

1

Table 1.1. Park units in the Northern Great Plains Network.

Acronym	Name
AGFO	Agate Fossil Beds National Monument
BADL	Badlands National Park
DETO	Devils Tower National Monument
FOLA	Fort Laramie National Historic Site
FOUS	Fort Union Trading Post National Historic Site
JECA	Jewel Cave National Monument
KNRI	Knife River Indian Villages National Historic Site
MNRR	Missouri National Recreational River
MORU	Mount Rushmore National Memorial
NIOB	Niobrara National Scenic Riverway
SCBL	Scotts Bluff National Monument
THRO	Theodore Roosevelt National Park
WICA	Wind Cave National Park

networks usually have additional inventory data and station-tracking procedures. Some national weather/climate networks are associated with the National Oceanic and Atmospheric Administration (NOAA), including the National Weather Service (NWS) Cooperative Observer Program (COOP). Other national networks include the interagency Remote Automated Weather Station network (RAWS) and the U.S. Department of Agriculture/Natural Resources Conservation Service (USDA/NRCS) Snowfall Telemetry (SNOTEL) and snowcourse networks. Usually a single agency, but sometimes a consortium of interested parties, will jointly support a particular weather/climate network.

1.1.2. NPS I&M Networks
Within the NPS, the system for monitoring various attributes in the participating park units (about 270–280 in total) is divided into 32 NPS I&M networks. These networks are collections of park units grouped together around a common theme, typically geographical.

1.2. Weather versus Climate Definitions
It is also important to distinguish whether the primary use of a given station is for weather purposes or for climate purposes. Weather station networks are intended for near-real-time usage, where the precise circumstances of a set of measurements are typically less important. In these cases, changes in exposure or other attributes over time are not as critical. Climate networks, however, are intended for long-term tracking of atmospheric conditions. Siting and exposure are critical factors for climate networks, and it is vitally important that the observational circumstances remain essentially unchanged over the duration of the station record.

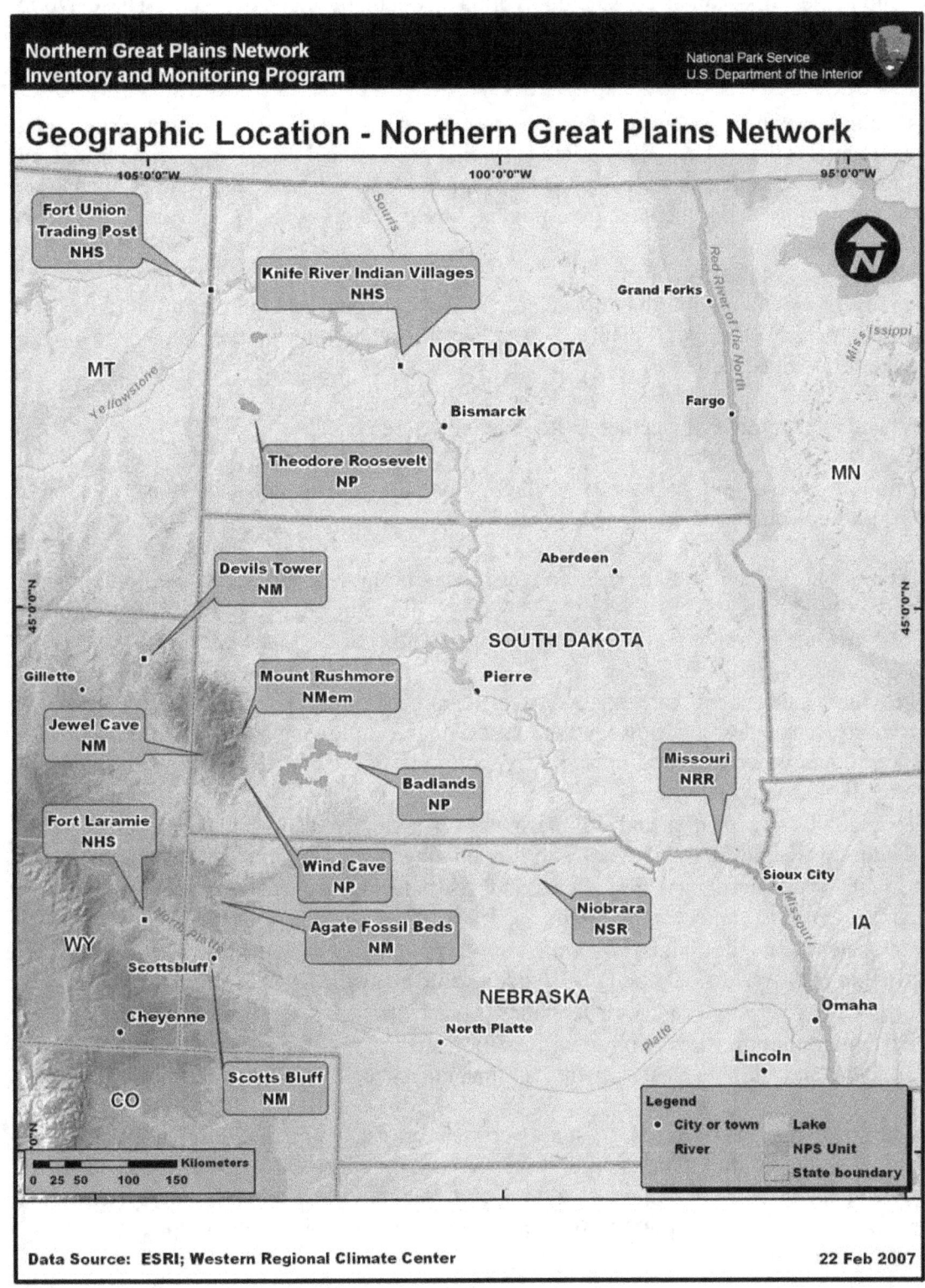

Figure 1.1. Map of the Northern Great Plains Network.

Some climate networks can be considered hybrids of weather/climate networks. These hybrid climate networks can supply information on a short-term "weather" time scale and a longer-term "climate" time scale.

In this report, "weather" generally refers to current (or near-real-time) atmospheric conditions, while "climate" is defined as the complete ensemble of statistical descriptors for temporal and spatial properties of atmospheric behavior (see Appendix A). Climate and weather phenomena shade gradually into each other and are ultimately inseparable.

1.3. Purpose of Measurements

Climate inventory and monitoring climate activities should be based on a set of guiding fundamental principles. Any evaluation of weather/climate monitoring programs begins with asking the following question:

- What is the purpose of weather and climate measurements?

Evaluation of past, present, or planned weather/climate monitoring activities must be based on the answer to this question.

Weather and climate data and information constitute a prominent and widely requested component of the NPS I&M networks (I&M 2006). Within the context of the NPS, the following services constitute the main purposes for recording weather and climate observations:

- Provide measurements for real-time operational needs and early warnings of potential hazards (landslides, mudflows, washouts, fallen trees, plowing activities, fire conditions, aircraft and watercraft conditions, road conditions, rescue conditions, fog, restoration and remediation activities, etc.).
- Provide visitor education and aid interpretation of expected and actual conditions for visitors while they are in the park and for deciding if and when to visit the park.
- Establish engineering and design criteria for structures, roads, culverts, etc., for human comfort, safety, and economic needs.
- Consistently monitor climate over the long-term to detect changes in environmental drivers affecting ecosystems, including both gradual and sudden events.
- Provide retrospective data to understand *a posteriori* changes in flora and fauna.
- Document for posterity the physical conditions in and near the park units, including mean, extreme, and variable measurements (in time and space) for all applications.

The last three items in the preceding list are pertinent primarily to the NPS I&M networks; however, all items are important to NPS operations and management. Most of the needs in this list overlap heavily. It is often impractical to operate separate climate measuring systems that also cannot be used to meet ordinary weather needs, where there is greater emphasis on timeliness and reliability.

1.4. Design of Climate-Monitoring Programs

Determining the purposes for collecting measurements in a given weather/climate monitoring program will guide the process of identifying weather/climate stations suitable for the monitoring program. The context for making these decisions is provided in Chapter 2 where background on the NGPN climate is presented. However, this process is only one step in evaluating and designing a climate-monitoring program. The following steps must also be included:

- Define park and network-specific monitoring needs and objectives.
- Identify locations and data repositories of existing and historic stations.
- Acquire existing data when necessary or practical.
- Evaluate the quality of existing data.
- Evaluate the adequacy of coverage of existing stations.
- Develop a protocol for monitoring the weather and climate, including the following:
  o Standardized summaries and reports of weather/climate data.
  o Data management (quality assurance and quality control, archiving, data access, etc.).
- Develop and implement a plan for installing or modifying stations, as necessary.

Throughout the design process, there are various factors that require consideration in evaluating weather and climate measurements. Many of these factors have been summarized by Dr. Tom Karl, director of the NOAA National Climatic Data Center (NCDC), and widely distributed as the "Ten Principles for Climate Monitoring" (Karl et al. 1996; NRC 2001). These principles are presented in Appendix B, and the guidelines are embodied in many of the comments made throughout this report. The most critical factors are presented here. In addition, an overview of requirements necessary to operate a climate network is provided in Appendix C, with further discussion in Appendix D.

1.4.1. Need for Consistency
A principal goal in climate monitoring is to detect and characterize slow and sudden changes in climate through time. This is of less concern for day-to-day weather changes, but it is of paramount importance for climate variability and change. There are many ways whereby changes in techniques for making measurements, changes in instruments or their exposures, or seemingly innocuous changes in site characteristics can lead to apparent changes in climate. Safeguards must be in place to avoid these false sources of temporal "climate" variability if we are to draw correct inferences about climate behavior over time from archived measurements.

For climate monitoring, consistency through time is vital, counting at least as important as absolute accuracy. Sensors record only what is occurring at the sensor—this is all they can detect. It is the responsibility of station or station network managers to ensure that observations are representative of the spatial and temporal climate scales that we wish to record.

1.4.2. Metadata
Changes in instruments, site characteristics, and observing methodologies can lead to apparent changes in climate through time. It is therefore vital to document all factors that can bear on the interpretation of climate measurements and to update the information repeatedly through time. This information ("metadata," data about data) has its own history and set of quality-control issues that parallel those of the actual data. There is no single standard for the content of climate metadata, but a simple rule suffices:

- Observers should record all information that could be needed in the future to interpret observations correctly without benefit of the observers' personal recollections.

Such documentation includes notes, drawings, site forms, and photos, which can be of inestimable value if taken in the correct manner. That stated, it is not always clear to the metadata provider *what is important* for posterity and *what will be important* in the future. It is almost impossible to "over document" a station. Station documentation is greatly underappreciated and is seldom thorough enough (especially for climate purposes). Insufficient attention to this issue often lowers the present and especially future value of otherwise useful data.

The convention followed throughout climatology is to refer to metadata as information about the measurement process, station circumstances, and data. The term "data" is reserved solely for the actual weather and climate records obtained from sensors.

1.4.3. Maintenance

Inattention to maintenance is the greatest source of failure in weather/climate stations and networks. Problems begin to occur soon after sites are deployed. A regular visit schedule must be implemented, where sites, settings (e.g., vegetation), sensors, communications, and data flow are checked routinely (once or twice a year at a minimum) and updated as necessary. Parts must be changed out for periodic recalibration or replacement. With adequate maintenance, the entire instrument suite should be replaced or completely refurbished about once every five to seven years.

Simple preventive maintenance is effective but requires much planning and skilled technical staff. Changes in technology and products require retraining and continual re-education. Travel, logistics, scheduling, and seasonal access restrictions consume major amounts of time and budget but are absolutely necessary. Without such attention, data gradually become less credible and then often are misused or not used at all.

1.4.4. Automated versus Manual Stations

Historic stations often have depended on manual observations and many continue to operate in this mode. Manual observations frequently produce excellent data sets. Sensors and data are simple and intuitive, well tested, and relatively cheap. Manual stations have much to offer in certain circumstances and can be a source of both primary and backup data. However, methodical consistency for manual measurements is a constant challenge, especially with a mobile work force. Operating manual stations takes time and needs to be done on a regular schedule, though sometimes the routine is welcome.

Nearly all newer stations are automated. Automated stations provide better time resolution, increased (though imperfect) reliability, greater capacity for data storage, and improved accessibility to large amounts of data. The purchase cost for automated stations is higher than for manual stations. A common expectation and serious misconception is that an automated station can be deployed and left to operate on its own. In reality, automation does not eliminate the need for people but rather changes the type of person that is needed. Skilled technical personnel are needed and must be readily available, especially if live communications exist and data gaps are not wanted. Site visits are needed at least annually and spare parts must be maintained. Typical annual costs for sensors and maintenance are $1500–2500 per station per year but these costs still can vary greatly depending on the kind of automated site.

1.4.5. Communications
With manual stations, the observer is responsible for recording and transmitting station data. Data from automated stations, however, can be transmitted quickly for access by research and operations personnel, which is a highly preferable situation. A comparison of communication systems for automated and manual stations shows that automated stations generally require additional equipment, more power, higher transmission costs, attention to sources of disruption or garbling, and backup procedures (e.g., manual downloads from data loggers).

Automated stations are capable of functioning normally without communication and retaining many months of data. At such sites, however, alerts about station problems are not possible, large gaps can accrue when accessible stations quit, and the constituencies needed to support such stations are smaller and less vocal. Two-way communications permit full recovery from disruptions, ability to reprogram data loggers remotely, and better opportunities for diagnostics and troubleshooting. In virtually all cases, two-way communications are much preferred to all other communication methods. However, two-way communications require considerations of cost, signal access, transmission rates, interference, and methods for keeping sensor and communication power loops separate. Two-way communications are frequently impossible (no service) or impractical, expensive, or power consumptive. Two-way methods (cellular, land line, radio, Internet) require smaller up-front costs as compared to other methods of communication and have variable recurrent costs, starting at zero. Satellite links work everywhere (except when blocked by trees or cliffs) and are quite reliable but are one-way and relatively slow, allow no re-transmissions, and require high up-front costs ($3000–4000) but no recurrent costs. Communications technology is changing constantly and requires vigilant attention by maintenance personnel.

1.4.6. Quality Assurance and Quality Control
Quality control and quality assurance are issues at every step through the entire sequence of sensing, communication, storage, retrieval, and display of environmental data. Quality assurance is an umbrella concept that covers all data collection and processing (start-to-finish) and ensures that credible information is available to the end user. Quality control has a more limited scope and is defined by the International Standards Organization as "the operational techniques and activities that are used to satisfy quality requirements." The central problem can be better appreciated if we approach quality control in the following way.

- Quality control is the evaluation, assessment, and rehabilitation of imperfect data by utilizing other imperfect data.

The quality of the data only decreases with time once the observation is made. The best and most effective quality control, therefore, consists in making high-quality measurements from the start and then successfully transmitting the measurements to an ingest process and storage site. Once the data are received from a monitoring station, a series of checks with increasing complexity can be applied, ranging from single-element checks (self-consistency) to multiple-element checks (inter-sensor consistency) to multiple-station/single-element checks (inter-station consistency). Suitable ancillary data (battery voltages, data ranges for all measurements, etc.) can prove extremely useful in diagnosing problems.

There is rarely a single technique in quality control procedures that will work satisfactorily for all situations. Quality-control procedures must be tailored to individual station circumstances, data access and storage methods, and climate regimes.

The fundamental issue in quality control centers on the tradeoff between falsely rejecting good data (Type I error) and falsely accepting bad data (Type II error). We cannot reduce the incidence of one type of error without increasing the incidence of the other type. In weather and climate data assessments, since good data are absolutely crucial for interpreting climate records properly, Type I errors are deemed far less desirable than Type II errors.

Not all observations are equal in importance. Quality-control procedures are likely to have the greatest difficulty evaluating the most extreme observations, where independent information usually must be sought and incorporated. Quality-control procedures involving more than one station usually involve a great deal of infrastructure with its own (imperfect) error-detection methods, which must be in place before a single value can be evaluated.

1.4.7. Standards
Although there is near-universal recognition of the value in systematic weather and climate measurements, these measurements will have little value unless they conform to accepted standards. There is not a single source for standards for collecting weather and climate data nor a single standard that meets all needs. Measurement standards have been developed by the World Meteorological Organization (WMO 1983; 2005), the American Association of State Climatologists (AASC 1985), the U.S. Environmental Protection Agency (EPA 1987), Finklin and Fischer (1990), the RAWS program (Bureau of Land Management [BLM] 1997), and the National Wildfire Coordinating Group (2004). Variations to these measurement standards also have been offered by instrument makers (e.g., Tanner 1990).

1.4.8. Who Makes the Measurements?
The lands under NPS stewardship provide many excellent locations to host the monitoring of climate by the NPS or other collaborators. These lands are largely protected from human development and other land changes that can impact observed climate records. Most park units historically have observed weather/climate elements as part of their overall mission. Many of these measurements come from station networks managed by other agencies, with observations taken or overseen by NPS personnel, in some cases, or by collaborators from the other agencies. Any NPS park units that are small, lack sufficient resources, or lack sites presenting adequate exposure may benefit by utilizing weather/climate measurements collected from nearby stations.

2.0. Climate Background

Climate is a primary driver of almost all physical and ecological processes in the NGPN (Licht et al. 2005). Conceptual ecosystem models for the NGPN have also emphasized the influence of climate on other Vital Signs in the region (Licht et al. 2005). An understanding of both current climate patterns and climate history in the NGPN is important to understanding and interpreting change and patterns in ecosystem attributes. It is essential that the NGPN park units have an effective climate monitoring system to track climate changes and to aid in management decisions relating to these changes. In order to do this, it is essential to understand the climate characteristics of the NGPN, as discussed in this chapter.

2.1. Climate and the NGPN Environment

In terms of climate the Northern Great Plains is classified as continental and is characterized by extremes in weather ranging from hot dry summers to cold winters with prolonged snow cover. Borchert (1950) summarized the common climatic attributes of North American prairie as 1) low winter snow and rainfall, 2) high probabilities of large rainfall deficits in summer (especially as it relates to primary production), 3) fewer days of rainfall compared to nearby forested areas, 4) low summer cloud cover, 5) low summer relative humidity, 6) large departures from average temperature, 7) frequent hot, dry winds in summer; and 8) frequent departures from average climatic conditions. There is great variability between days, seasons, and years in Great Plains climate (Licht et al. 2005). According to Wilken (1988) the dramatic weather extremes in the Great Plains are really part of the "normal" events for the region. Severely harsh winters with long periods of snow cover occur periodically and can cause significant mortality for some wildlife (Licht et al. 2005). Precipitation, which can occur either as rain or snow, is quite variable interannually (Whiteman 1973; Mock 1991; Bunkers et al. 1996) and occurs largely in association with infrequent, heavy convective storms, especially in the spring and summer. The Great Plains regularly goes through multi-year droughts on a cycle that has ranged from 10-20 years over the past few centuries (Clark et al. 2002; Schubert et al. 2004; Shapley et al. 2005) However, pre-Columbian cycles may have lasted much longer (Clark et al. 2002).

The variable climate in the NGPN is a driving influence on the composition, structure, and processes of prairie ecosystems (Ji and Peters 2003), and directly affects other primary drivers of NGPN ecosystems (Licht et al. 2005). For instance, during and after the Dust Bowl of the 1930s, Weaver (1943) found significant eastward shifts in the mixed-grass prairie biome. Although droughts are typically viewed as a negative impact on grasslands, that is a commodity or economic perspective. From an ecological viewpoint droughts are a primary force in maintaining grassland communities (Clark et al. 2002; Licht et al. 2005). High winds compound the effects of temperature and precipitation, and have numerous less subtle but equally important effects on the ecosystem (e.g., pollen and seed dispersal). The high variability of NGPN climate easily confounds efforts to analyze and interpret temporal and spatial trends and to identify causative factors in changes in natural resources. Since NGPN climate shows large variations, both spatially and especially temporally, the NGPN network has stressed the importance of site-specific weather and climate monitoring for accurate results (Licht et al. 2005).

The impact of global climate change may be exacerbated in the Northern Great Plains due to the region's periodic droughts and the large number of habitat specialists (Collins and Glenn 1995;

Ojima et al. 1999; Clark et al. 2002). Anthropogenic climate change could significantly affect weather patterns in the Great Plains. A warmer and more arid Great Plains due to climate warming could paradoxically result in a shift to more C3 (i.e., cool season) plants because these plants can better exploit what little moisture is available in the spring before the severe water deficits of summer (Clark et al. 2002). However, other analyses (e.g., Collins and Glenn 1995) suggest a change to more C4 plants. Climate change may affect not only the means, but the variability in weather patterns, perhaps resulting in longer drought cycles. A modeling study of climate change on WICA found that global warming could increase grassland vegetation and decrease forested and shrubby vegetation (Bachelet 2000).

2.2. Spatial Variability

Precipitation in the NGPN region is generally light to moderate, increasing from west to east across the network (Licht et al. 2005). Superimposed on this general pattern is a smaller area of higher precipitation which occurs in the Black Hills of South Dakota (Figure 2.1). Mean annual precipitation ranges from under 400 mm in park units such as FOUS and FOLA, to over 600 mm in eastern portions of MNRR. Mean annual snowfall across the NGPN is fairly uniform, with the exception of much higher totals in the Black Hills. While much of the NGPN sees mean annual snowfalls of 50-100 cm, portions of the Black Hills can regularly receive over 400 cm (Figure 2.2). The snowiest NGPN park units (e.g., DETO and JECA) are generally located in or near the Black Hills and receive well over 100 cm of snowfall each year. In contrast, less than 75 cm of snow are generally received each year in MNRR, in the eastern portions of the NGPN network. Precipitation in NGPN park units generally peaks in late spring or early summer (Figure 2.3), primarily in associated with convective thunderstorm events. This seasonal peak in precipitation is sharper in western NGPN than in eastern NGPN.

Mean annual temperatures across the NGPN generally increase from north to south, with cooler conditions in the Black Hills superimposed on that gradient (Figure 2.4). The coldest conditions are found in central North Dakota, including KNRI, where mean annual temperatures are below 5°C. In contrast, mean annual temperatures in southern NGPN park units exceed 7°C, with the warmest temperatures at BADL approaching 9°C or greater. The north-south temperature gradient is also apparent when looking at winter minimum (e.g., Figure 2.5) and summer maximum (e.g., Figure 2.6) temperatures. Winter minimum temperatures also show an east-west gradient, with temperatures decreasing from west to east. The mildest park units are located closest to the Rocky Mountains and are influenced more frequently by warming downslope winds coming off the Rocky Mountain chain. The NGPN park units in the eastern portions of the Black Hills (e.g., MORU, WICA) also are exposed regularly to these downslope winds and have some of the mildest winter temperatures in the NGPN (with January minimum temperatures around 10°C). The coldest winter temperatures occur in North Dakota park units (e.g., FOUS and KNRI), where January minimum temperatures commonly approach -20°C. Summer maximum temperatures are quite warm throughout the NGPN. For example, much of the network averages between 27 and 33°C for July maximum temperatures. Not surprisingly, the warmest conditions are found in southern NGPN. The higher elevations of the Black Hills experience much cooler summertime temperatures compared to their surroundings. Both JECA and MORU have average July maximum temperatures that are at or just below 27°C, while the higher elevations to the north and west can even be several degrees cooler. Superimposed on

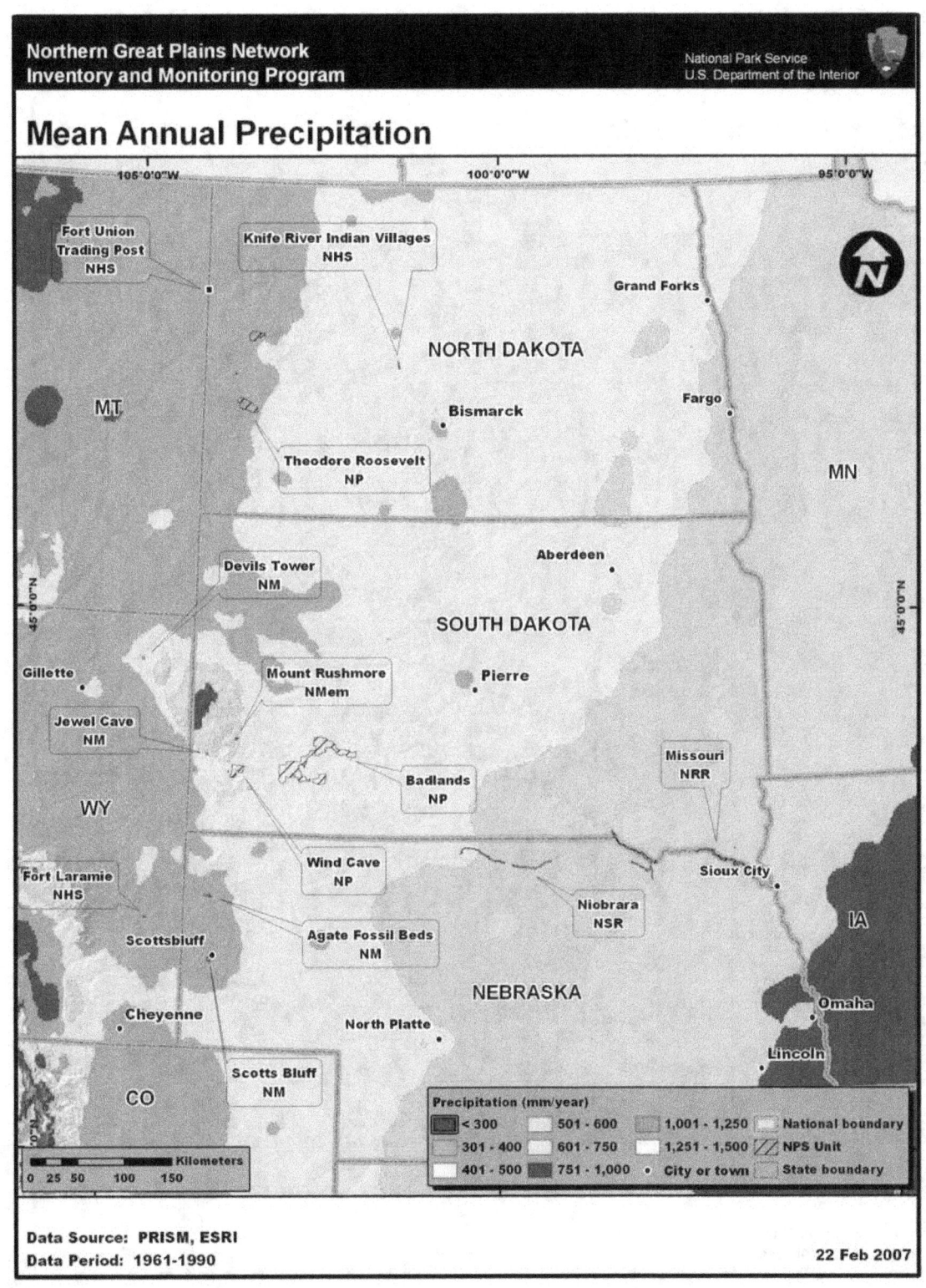

Figure 2.1. Mean annual precipitation, 1961-1990, for the NGPN.

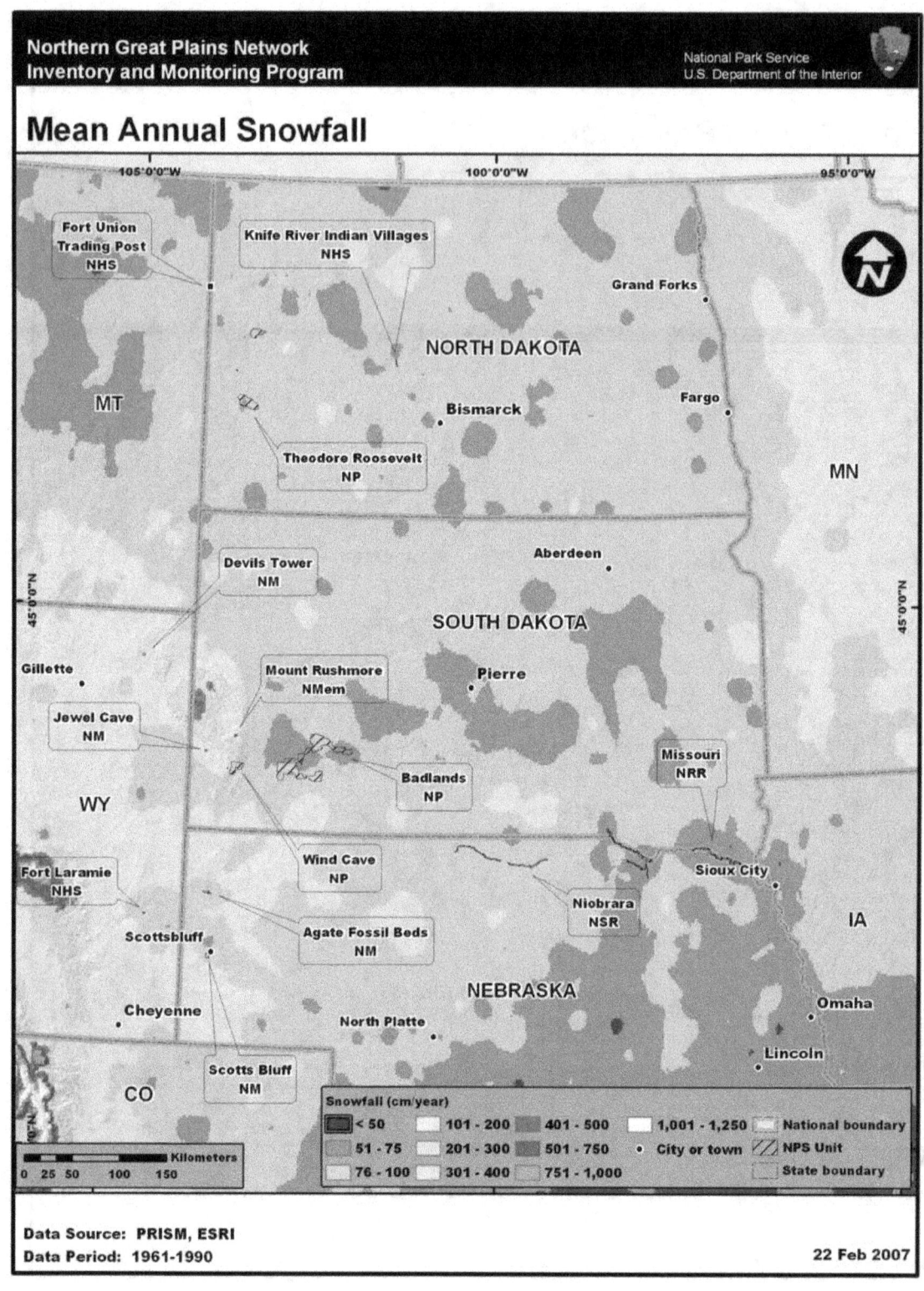

Figure 2.2. Mean annual snowfall, 1961-1990, for the NGPN.

a)

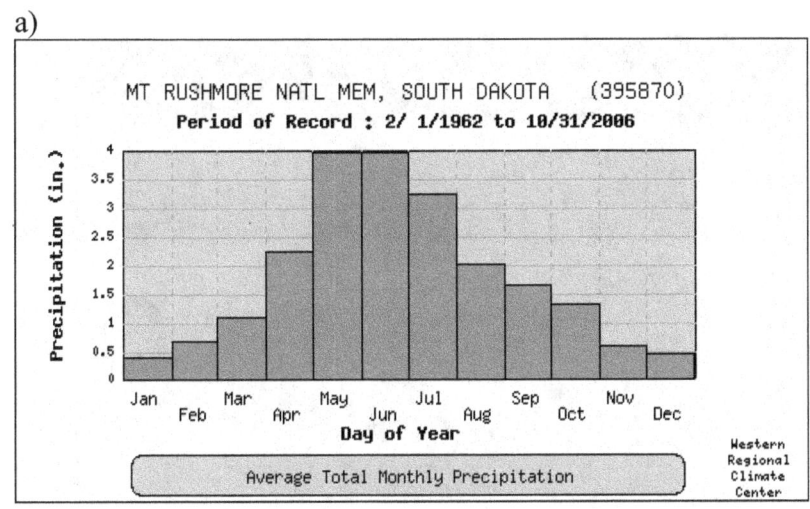

b)

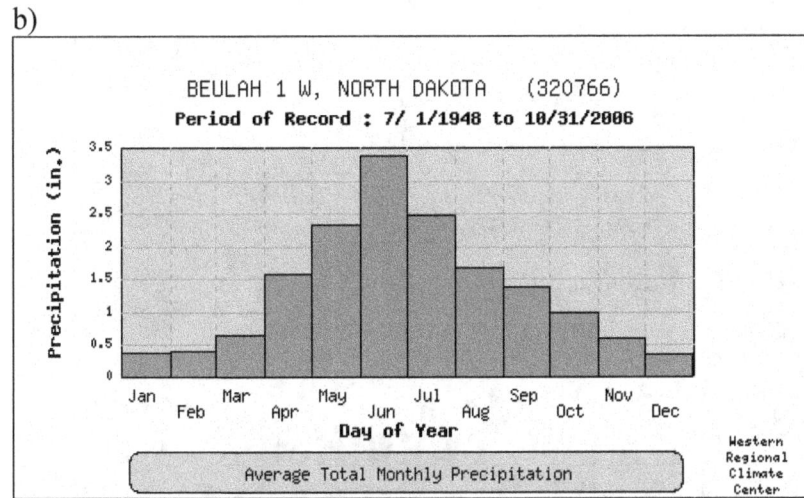

c)

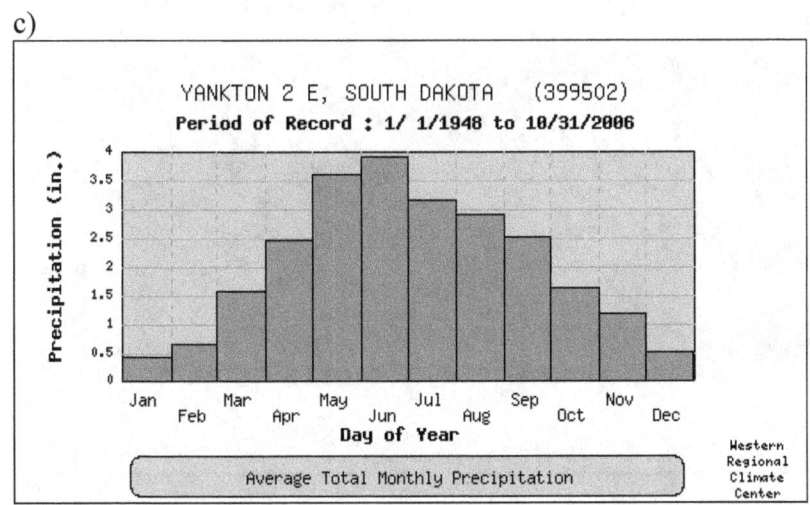

Figure 2.3. Mean monthly precipitation at selected locations in the NGPN, including MORU (a); Beulah 1 W, near KNRI (b), and Yankton 2 E, near MNRR (c).

13

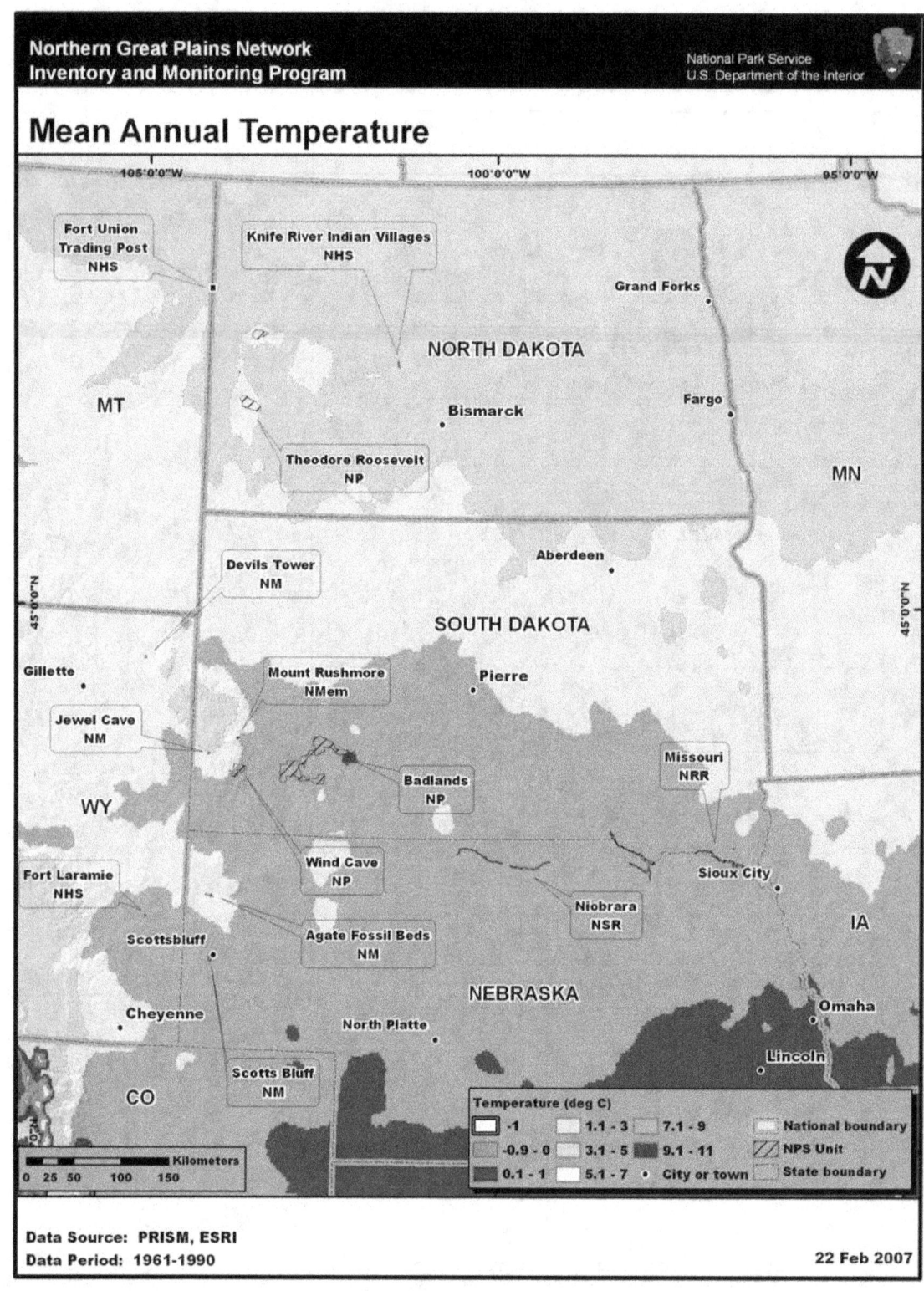

Figure 2.4. Mean annual temperature, 1961-1990, for the NGPN.

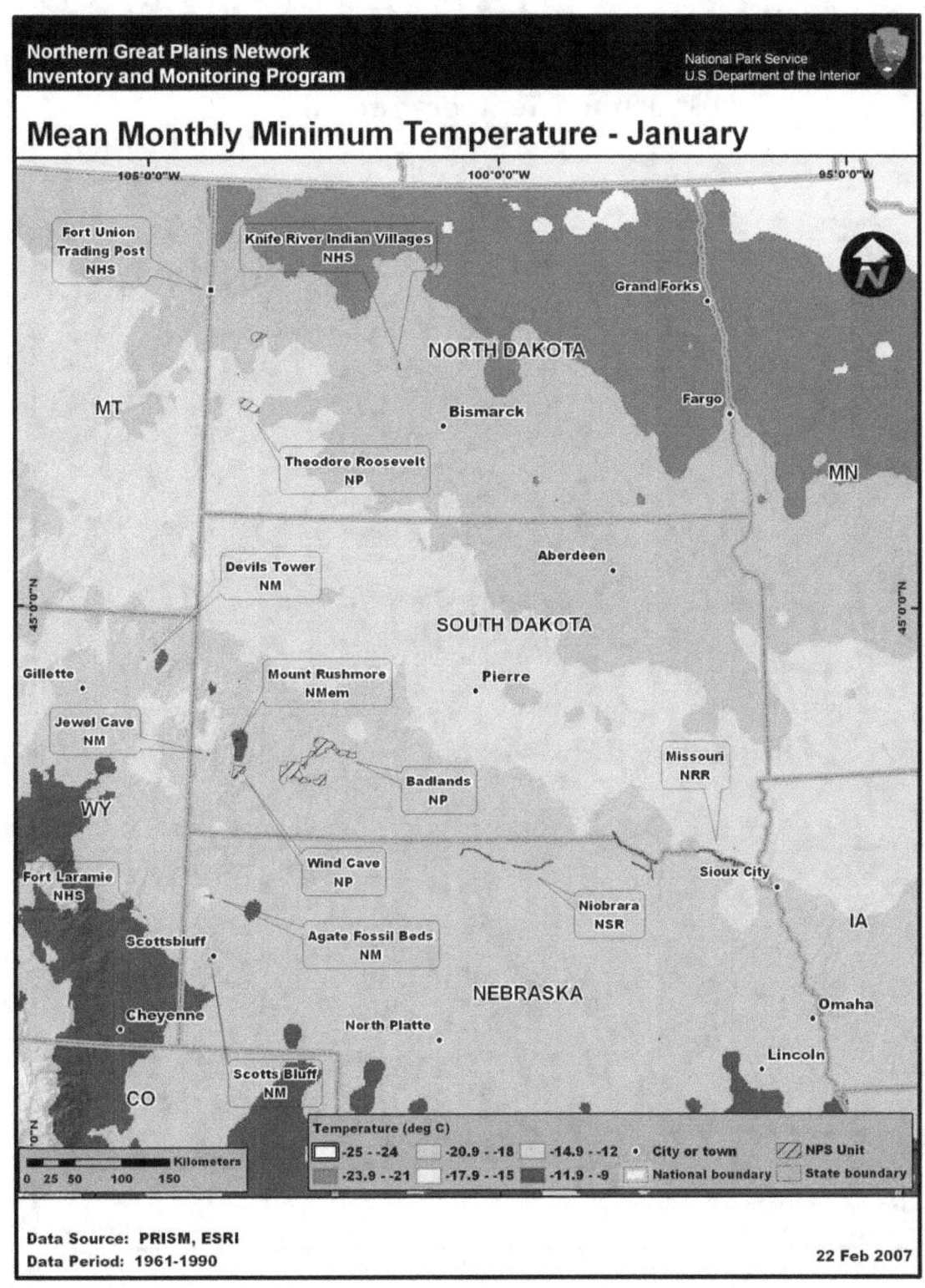

Figure 2.5. Mean January minimum temperature, 1961-1990, for the NGPN.

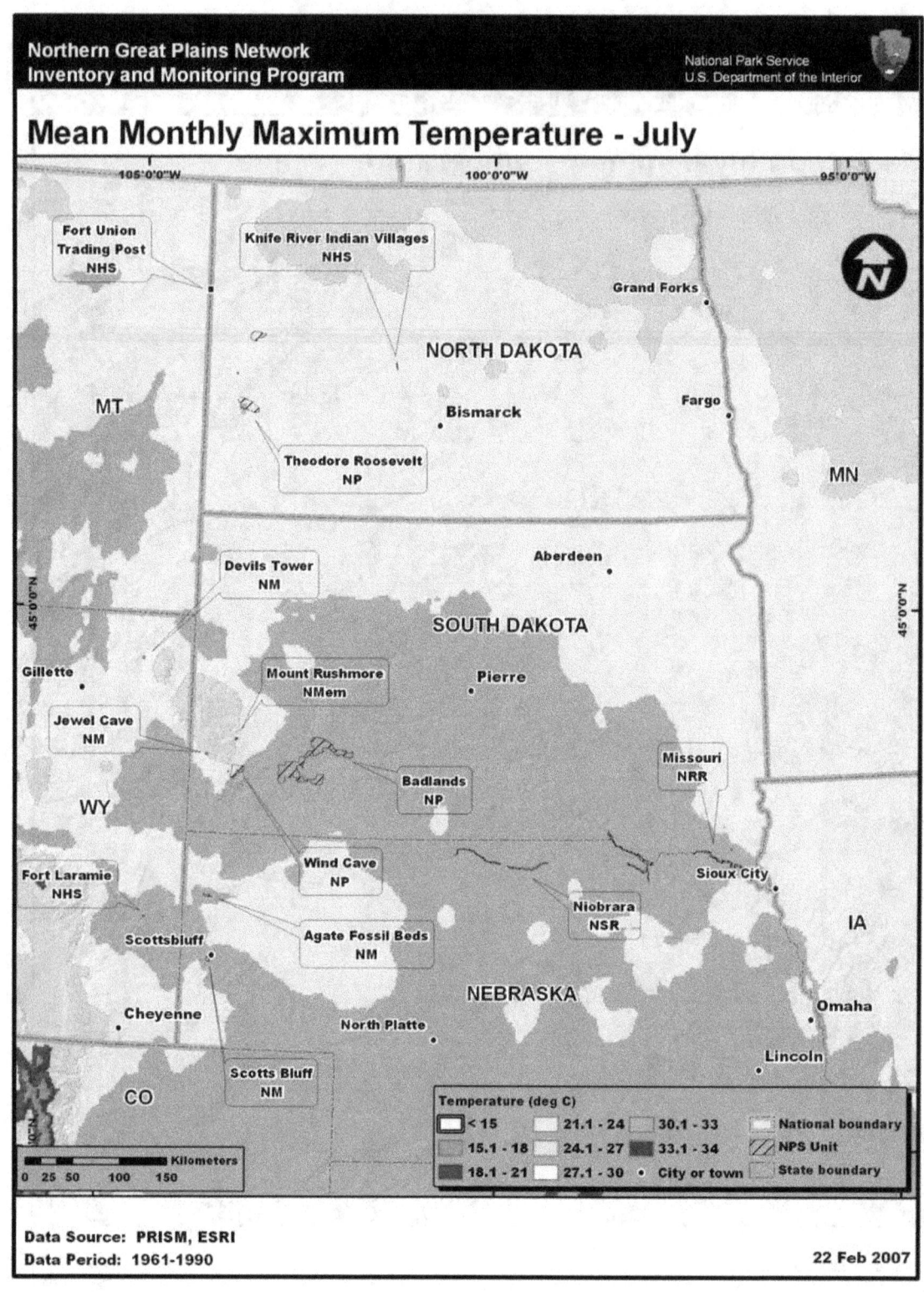

Figure 2.6. Mean July maximum temperature, 1961-1990, for the NGPN.

these larger-scale temperature patterns are local-scale variations caused by local topographical features such as river drainages. These local variations are especially evident for overnight minimum temperatures, as cold-air drainages set up in park units like AFGO, MNRR, and THRO, keeping temperatures here much lower than at adjacent locations on the surrounding plains.

2.3. Temporal Variability

As previously discussed, the NGPN climate displays significant temporal variability at scales ranging from days to years. A significant driver of the interannual climate variations in the NGPN is the El Niño-Southern Oscillation, or ENSO (Bunkers et al. 1996; NAST 2001). Generally, El Niño conditions (warm ENSO phases) are associated with warmer and drier conditions while La Niña conditions (cool ENSO phases) are associated with cooler and wetter conditions.

An investigation of precipitation time series around the NGPN region over the last century (Figure 2.7) reveals mixed results. Precipitation over southern and western portions of NGPN has been neutral or decreased slightly (e.g., Figure 2.7a) during the past century. In contrast to this, southeastern South Dakota (Figure 2.7c) has shown a slight increase in precipitation during the past century. In all of these time series, the drier period during the 1930s is readily apparent, as are the drier conditions that have occurred in the region since the late 1990s.

Long-term temperature trends in the NGPN (Figure 2.8) indicate a steady warming trend in the past 3-4 decades. After strong warming in the first part of the twentieth century, cooling trends were evident across the NGPN from the 1950s through the 1970s. After the 1970s, steady warming has occurred in the region.

2.4. Parameter Regression on Independent Slopes Model

The climate maps presented in this report were generated using the Parameter Regression on Independent Slopes Model (PRISM). This model was developed to address the extreme spatial and elevation gradients exhibited by U.S. climate. (Daly et al. 1994; 2002; Gibson et al. 2002; Doggett et al. 2004). The maps produced through PRISM have undergone rigorous evaluation for the entire U.S. This model was originally developed to provide climate information at scales matching available land-cover maps to assist in ecologic modeling. The PRISM technique accounts for the scale-dependent effects of topography on mean values of climate elements. Elevation provides the first-order constraint for the mapped climate fields, with slope and orientation (aspect) providing second-order constraints. The model has been enhanced gradually to address inversions, coast/land gradients, and climate patterns in small-scale trapping basins. Monthly climate fields are generated by PRISM to account for seasonal variations in elevation gradients in climate elements. These monthly climate fields then can be combined into seasonal and annual climate fields. Since PRISM maps are grid maps, they do not replicate point values but rather, for a given grid cell, represent the grid-cell average of the climate variable in question at the average elevation for that cell. The model relies on observed surface and upper-air measurements to estimate spatial climate fields.

a)

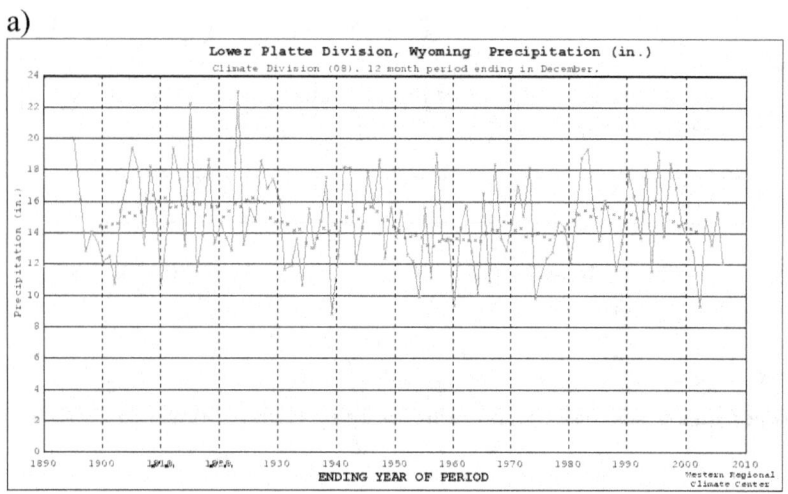

b)

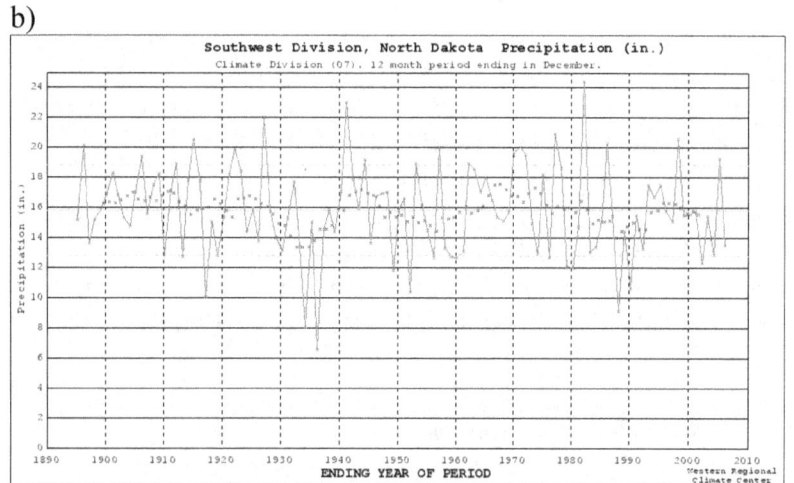

c)

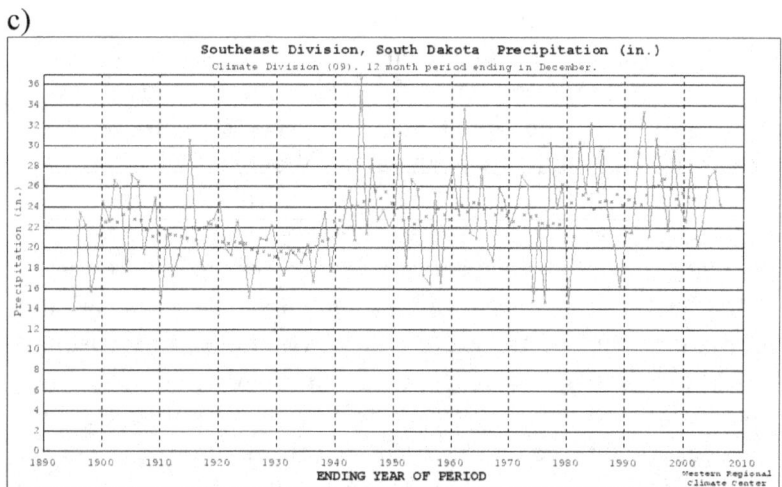

Figure 2.7. Precipitation time series, 1895-2005, for selected regions in the NGPN. These include twelve-month precipitation (ending in December) (red), 10-year running mean (blue), mean (green), and plus/minus one standard deviation (green dotted). Locations include southeastern Wyoming (a), southwestern North Dakota (b), and southeastern South Dakota (c).

18

a)

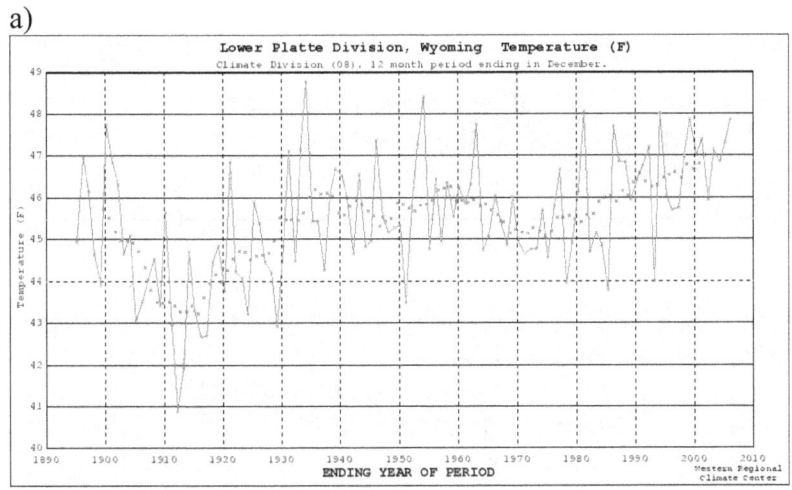

b)

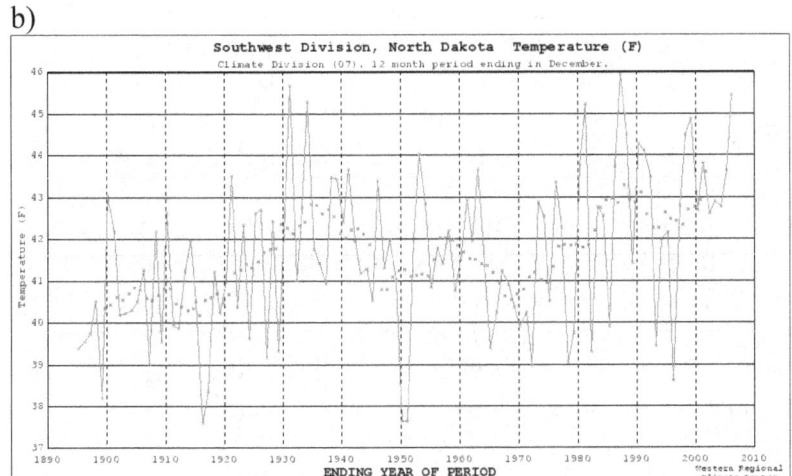

c)

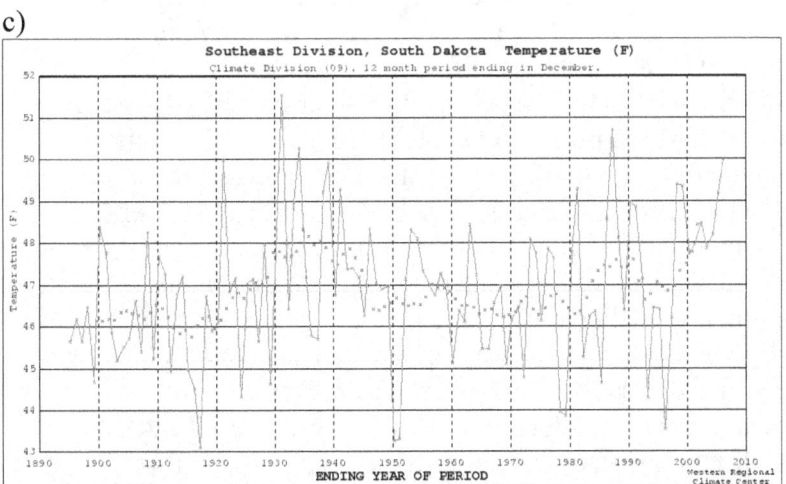

Figure 2.8. Temperature time series, 1895-2005, for selected regions in the NGPN. These include twelve-month average temperature (ending in December) (red), 10-year running mean (blue), mean (green), and plus/minus one standard deviation (green dotted). Locations include southeastern Wyoming (a), southwestern North Dakota (b), and southeastern South Dakota (c).

19

3.0. Methods

Having discussed the climatic characteristics of the NGPN, we now present the procedures that were used to obtain information for weather and climate stations within the NGPN. This information was obtained from various sources, as mentioned in the following paragraphs. Retrieval of station metadata constituted a major component of this work.

3.1. Metadata Retrieval

A key component of station inventories is determining the kinds of observations that have been conducted over time, by whom, and in what manner; when each type of observation began and ended; and whether these observations are still being conducted. Metadata about the observational process (Table 3.1) generally consist of a series of vignettes that apply to time intervals and, therefore, constitute a *history* rather than a single snapshot. An expanded list of relevant metadata fields for this inventory is provided in Appendix E. This report has relied on metadata records from three sources: (a) Western Regional Climate Center (WRCC), (b) NPS personnel, and (c) other knowledgeable personnel, such as state climate office staff.

The initial metadata sources for this report were stored at WRCC. This regional climate center (RCC) acts as a working repository of many western climate records, including the main networks outlined in this section. The WRCC conducts live and periodic data collection (ingests) from all major national and western weather and climate networks. These networks include the COOP network, the Surface Airways Observation network (SAO) operated by NWS and the Federal Aviation Administration (FAA), the interagency RAWS network, and various smaller networks. The WRCC is expanding its capability to ingest information from other networks as resources permit and usefulness dictates. This center has relied heavily on historic archives (in many cases supplemented with live ingests) to assess the quantity (not necessarily quality) of data available for NPS I&M network applications.

The primary source of metadata at WRCC is the Applied Climate Information System (ACIS), a joint effort among RCCs and other NOAA entities. Metadata for NGPN weather/climate stations identified from the ACIS database are available in file "NGPN_from_ACIS.tar.gz" (see Appendix F). Historic metadata pertaining to major climate- and weather-observing systems in the U.S. are stored in ACIS where metadata are linked to the observed data. A distributed system, ACIS is synchronized among the RCCs. Mainstream software is utilized, including Postgress, Python™, and Java™ programming languages; CORBA®-compliant network software; and industry-standard, nonproprietary hardware and software. Metadata and data for all major national climate and weather networks have been entered into the ACIS database. For this project, the available metadata from many smaller networks also have been entered but in most cases the actual data have not yet been entered. Data sets are in the NetCDF (Network Common Data Form) format, but the design allows for integration with legacy systems, including non-NetCDF files (used at WRCC) and additional metadata (added for this project). The ACIS also supports a suite of products to visualize or summarize data from these data sets. National climate-monitoring maps are updated daily using the ACIS data feed. The developmental phases of ACIS have utilized metadata supplied by the NCDC and NWS with many tens of thousands of entries, screened as well as possible for duplications, mistakes, and omissions.

Table 3.1. Primary metadata fields for NGPN weather and climate stations. Explanations are provided as appropriate.

Metadata Field	Notes
Station name	Station name associated with network listed in "Climate Network."
Latitude	Numerical value (units: see coordinate units).
Longitude	Numerical value (units: see coordinate units).
Coordinate units	Latitude/longitude (units: decimal degrees, degree-minute-second, etc.).
Datum	Datum used as basis for coordinates: WGS 84, NAD 83, etc.
Elevation	Elevation of station above mean sea level (m).
Slope	Slope of ground surface below station (degrees).
Aspect	Azimuth that ground surface below station faces.
Climate division	NOAA climate division where station is located. Climate divisions are NOAA-specified zones sharing similar climate and hydrology characteristics.
Country	Country where station is located.
State	State where station is located.
County	County where station is located.
Weather/climate network	Primary weather/climate network the station belongs to (COOP, RAWS, etc.).
NPS unit code	Four-letter code identifying park unit where station resides.
NPS unit name	Full name of park unit.
NPS unit type	National park, national monument, etc.
UTM zone	If UTM is the only coordinate system available.
Location notes	Useful information not already included in "station narrative."
Climate variables	Temperature, precipitation, etc.
Installation date	Date of station installation.
Removal date	Date of station removal.
Station photograph	Digital image of station.
Photograph date	Date photograph was taken.
Photographer	Name of person who took the photograph.
Station narrative	Anything related to general site description; may include site exposure, characteristics of surrounding vegetation, driving directions, etc.
Contact name	Name of the person involved with station operation.
Organization	Group or agency affiliation of contact person.
Contact type	Designation that identifies contact person as the station owner, observer, maintenance person, data manager, etc.
Position/job title	Official position/job title of contact person.
Address	Address of contact person.
E-mail address	E-mail address of contact person.
Phone	Phone number of contact person (and extension if available).
Contact notes	Other information needed to reach contact person.

In addition to obtaining NGPN weather and climate station metadata from ACIS, metadata were obtained from NPS staff at the NGPN office and are available in file "NGPN_NPS.tar.gz" (see Appendix F). Most of the stations noted by NGPN staff are already accounted for in ACIS.

Two types of information have been used to complete the NGPN weather and climate station inventory.

- Station inventories: Information about observational procedures, latitude/longitude, elevation, measured elements, measurement frequency, sensor types, exposures, ground cover and vegetation, data-processing details, network, purpose, and managing individual or agency, etc.

- Data inventories: Information about measured data values including completeness, seasonality, data gaps, representation of missing data, flagging systems, how special circumstances in the data record are denoted, etc.

This is not a straightforward process. Extensive searches are typically required to develop historic station and data inventories. Both types of inventories frequently contain information gaps and often rely on tacit and unrealistic assumptions. Sources of information for these inventories frequently are difficult to recover or are undocumented and unreliable. In many cases, the actual weather/climate data available from different sources are not linked directly to metadata records. To the extent that actual data can be acquired (rather than just metadata), it is possible to cross-check these records and perform additional assessments based on the amount and completeness of the data.

Certain types of weather or climate networks that possess any of the following attributes have not been considered for inclusion in the inventory:

- Private networks with proprietary access and/or inability to provide sufficient metadata.
- Private weather enthusiasts (often with high-quality data) whose metadata are not available and whose data are not readily accessible.
- Unofficial observers supplying data to the NWS (lack of access to current data and historic archives; lack of metadata).
- Networks having no available historic data.
- Networks having poor-quality metadata.
- Networks having poor access to metadata.
- Real-time networks having poor access to real-time data.

Previous inventory efforts at WRCC have shown that for the networks identified in the preceding list, in light of the need for quality data to track weather and climate, the resources required and difficulty encountered in obtaining metadata or data are prohibitively large.

3.2. Criteria for Locating Stations

To identify weather and climate stations for each park unit in the NGPN we selected only those stations located within 40 km of the NGPN park units. This buffer distance was selected in an attempt to include automated stations from major networks such as RAWS and SAO, but also to keep the size of the stations lists down to a reasonable number. The station locator maps presented in Chapter 4 were designed to show clearly the spatial distributions of all major weather/climate station networks in NGPN. We recognize that other mapping formats may be more suitable for other specific needs.

4.0. Station Inventory

An objective of this report is to show the locations of weather/climate stations for the NGPN region in relation to the boundaries of the NPS park units within the NGPN. A station does not have to be within park boundaries to provide useful data and information for a park unit.

4.1. Climate and Weather Networks

Most stations in the NGPN region are associated with at least one of 17 major weather and climate networks (Table 4.1). Brief descriptions of each weather/climate network are provided below (see Appendix G for greater detail).

Table 4.1. Weather and climate networks represented within the NGPN.

Acronym	Name
AWDN	Automated Weather Data Network
CASTNet	Clean Air Status and Trends Network
COOP	NWS Cooperative Observer Program
CRN	NOAA Climate Reference Network
CWOP	Citizen Weather Observer Program
GPMP	NPS Gaseous Pollutant Monitoring Program
GPS-MET	NOAA ground-based GPS meteorology network
MT DOT	Montana Department of Transportation network
NADP	National Atmospheric Deposition Program
NRCS-SC	USDA/NRCS snowcourse network
RAWS	Remote Automated Weather Station network
SAO	NWS/FAA Surface Airways Observation network
SCAN	Soil Climate Analysis Network
SNOTEL	USDA/NRCS Snowfall Telemetry network
UPR	Union Pacific Railroad network
WX4U	Weather For You network
WYDOT	Wyoming Department of Transportation network

4.1.1. Automated Weather Data Network (AWDN)

The High Plains Regional Climate Center (HPRCC) operates the AWDN network, which was initiated to provide denser coverage of near-real-time weather data for the Northern Great Plains. Hourly data are recorded for air temperature and humidity, soil temperature, wind speed and direction, solar radiation, and precipitation.

4.1.2. Clean Air Status and Trends Network (CASTNet)

CASTNet is primarily an air-quality monitoring network managed by the EPA. Standard hourly weather and climate elements are measured and include temperature, wind, humidity, solar radiation, soil temperature, and sometimes soil moisture. These elements are intended to support interpretation of air-quality parameters that also are measured at CASTNet sites. Data records at CASTNet sites are generally one–two decades in length.

4.1.3. NWS Cooperative Observer Program (COOP)

The COOP network has been a foundation of the U.S. climate program for decades and continues to play an important role. Manual measurements are made by volunteers and consist of daily maximum and minimum temperatures, observation-time temperature, daily precipitation, daily snowfall, and snow depth. When blended with NWS measurements, the data set is known as SOD, or "Summary of the Day." The quality of data from COOP sites ranges from excellent to modest.

4.1.4. NOAA Climate Reference Network (CRN)

The CRN is intended as a reference network for the U.S. that meets the requirements of the Global Climate Observing System. Up to 115 CRN sites are planned for installation, but the actual number of installed sites will depend on available funding. Standard meteorological elements are measured. CRN data are used in operational climate-monitoring activities and to place current climate patterns in historic perspective.

4.1.5. Citizen Weather Observer Program (CWOP)

The CWOP network consists primarily of automated weather stations operated by private citizens who have either an Internet connection and/or a wireless Ham radio setup. Data from CWOP stations are specifically intended for use in research, education, and homeland security activities. Although standard meteorological elements such as temperature, precipitation, and wind are measured at all CWOP stations, station characteristics do vary, including sensor types and site exposure.

4.1.6. Gaseous Pollutant Monitoring Program (GPMP)

The GPMP network measures hourly meteorological data in support of pollutant monitoring activities. Measured elements include temperature, precipitation, humidity, wind, solar radiation, and surface wetness. These data are generally of high quality, with records extending up to two decades in length.

4.1.7. NOAA Ground-Based GPS Meteorology (GPS-MET)

The GPS-MET network is the first network of its kind dedicated to GPS (Global Positioning System) meteorology (see Duan et al. 1996). GPS meteorology utilizes the radio signals broadcast by the satellite Global Positioning System for atmospheric remote sensing. GPS meteorology applications have evolved along two paths: ground-based (Bevis et al. 1992) and space-based (Yuan et al. 1993). For more information, please see Appendix G. The stations identified in this inventory are all ground-based. The GPS-MET network was developed in response to the need for improved moisture observations to support weather forecasting, climate monitoring, and other research activities. The primary goals of this network are to measure atmospheric water vapor using ground-based GPS receivers, facilitate the operational use of these data, and encourage usage of GPS meteorology for atmospheric research and other applications. GPS-MET is a collaboration between NOAA and several other governmental and university organizations and institutions. Ancillary meteorological observations at GPS-MET stations include temperature, relative humidity, and barometric pressure.

4.1.8. Montana Department of Transportation (MT DOT)

These weather stations are operated by MT DOT in support of management activities for Montana's transportation network. Measured meteorological elements generally include temperature, precipitation, wind, and relative humidity.

4.1.9. National Atmospheric Deposition Program (NADP)

The purpose of the NADP network is to monitor primarily wet deposition at selected sites around the U.S. and its territories. The network is a collaborative effort among several agencies including USDA and the U.S. Geological Survey (USGS). Precipitation is the primary climate parameter measured at NADP sites. This network includes Mercury Deposition Network (MDN) sites.

4.1.10. USDA/NRCS Snowcourse Network (NRCS-SC)

The USDA/NRCS maintains a network of snow-monitoring stations known as snowcourses. These are all manual sites, measuring only snow depth and snow water content one–two times per month during the months of January to June. Data records for these snowcourses often extend back to the 1920s or 1930s, and the data are generally of high quality. Many of these sites have been replaced by SNOTEL sites, but several hundred snowcourses are still in operation.

4.1.11. Remote Automated Weather Station (RAWS) Network

The RAWS network is administered through many land management agencies, particularly the BLM and the Forest Service. Hourly meteorology elements are measured and include temperature, wind, humidity, solar radiation, fuel temperature, and precipitation (when temperatures are above freezing). The fire community is the primary client for RAWS data. These sites are remote and data typically are transmitted via GOES (Geostationary Operational Environmental Satellite). Some sites operate all winter. Most data records for RAWS sites began during or after the mid-1980s.

4.1.12. NWS Surface Airways Observation Network (SAO)

These stations are located usually at major airports and military bases. Almost all SAO sites are automated. The hourly data measured at these sites include temperature, precipitation, humidity, wind, barometric pressure, sky cover, ceiling, visibility, and current weather. Most data records begin during or after the 1940s, and these data are generally of high quality.

4.1.13. USDA/NRCS Soil Climate Analysis Network (SCAN)

The SCAN network is administered by NRCS and is intended to be a comprehensive nationwide soil moisture and climate information system to be used in supporting natural resource assessments and other conservation activities. These stations are usually located in the agricultural areas of the U.S. All SCAN sites are automated. The parameters measured at these sites include air temperature, precipitation, humidity, wind, barometric pressure, solar radiation, snow depth, and snow water content.

4.1.14. USDA/NRCS Snowfall Telemetry (SNOTEL) Network

The USDA/NRCS maintains a network of automated snow-monitoring stations known as SNOTEL. The network was implemented originally to measure daily precipitation and snow water content. Many modern SNOTEL sites now record hourly data, with some sites now recording temperature and snow depth. Most data records began during or after the mid-1970s.

4.1.15. Union Pacific Railroad Network (UPR)
This is a network of weather stations managed by UPR to support their shipping and transport activities, primarily in the central and western U.S. These stations are generally located along the UPR's main railroad lines. Measured meteorological elements include temperature, precipitation, wind, and relative humidity.

4.1.16. Weather For You Network (WX4U)
The WX4U network is a nationwide collection of weather stations run by local observers. Data quality varies with site. Standard meteorological elements are measured and usually include temperature, precipitation, wind, and humidity.

4.1.17. Wyoming Department of Transportation (WYDOT)
These weather stations are operated by WYDOT in support of management activities for Wyoming's transportation network. Measured meteorological elements generally include temperature, precipitation, wind, and relative humidity.

4.1.18. Weather Bureau Army Navy (WBAN)
Some stations are identified in this report as WBAN stations. This is a station identification system rather than a true weather/climate network. Stations identified with WBAN are largely historical stations that reported meteorological observations on the WBAN weather observation forms that were common during the early and middle parts of the twentieth century. The use of WBAN numbers to identify stations was one of the first attempts in the U.S. to use a coordinated station numbering scheme between several weather station networks, such as the COOP and SAO networks.

4.1.19. Other Networks
In addition to the major networks mentioned above, there are various networks that are operated for specific purposes by specific organizations or governmental agencies or scientific research projects. These networks could be present within NGPN but have not been identified in this report. Some of the commonly used networks include the following:

- NOAA upper-air stations
- U.S. Department of Energy Surface Radiation Budget Network (Surfrad)
- Park-specific-monitoring networks and stations
- Other research or project networks having many possible owners

4.2. Station Locations
The major weather/climate networks in the NGPN (discussed in Section 4.1) each have at most a few stations at or inside each park unit (Table 4.2). Most of these are COOP stations.

Lists of stations have been compiled for the NGPN. As previously mentioned, a station does not have to be within the boundaries to provide useful data and information regarding the park unit in question. Some might be physically *within* the administrative or political boundaries, whereas others might be just outside, or even some distance away, but would be *nearby* in terms of behavior and representativeness. What constitutes "useful" and "representative" are also significant questions, whose answers can vary according to application, type of element, period of record, procedural or methodological observation conventions, and the like.

Table 4.2. Number of stations within or nearby NGPN park units. Numbers are listed by park unit and by weather/climate network. Figures in parentheses indicate the numbers of stations within park boundaries.

Network	AGFO	BADL	DETO	FOLA	FOUS	JECA	KNRI
AWDN	0(0)	4(0)	0(0)	2(0)	3(0)	1(0)	1(0)
CASTNet	0(0)	0(0)	0(0)	0(0)	0(0)	1(0)	0(0)
COOP	10(1)	24(1)	16(2)	17(2)	15(0)	23(0)	12(0)
CRN	1(1)	0(0)	0(0)	0(0)	0(0)	0(0)	0(0)
CWOP	0(0)	3(0)	0(0)	0(0)	0(0)	0(0)	1(0)
GPMP	0(0)	2(2)	0(0)	0(0)	0(0)	0(0)	0(0)
GPS-MET	0(0)	0(0)	0(0)	0(0)	0(0)	0(0)	0(0)
MT DOT	0(0)	0(0)	0(0)	0(0)	2(0)	0(0)	0(0)
NADP	0(0)	1(0)	0(0)	0(0)	0(0)	2(0)	0(0)
NRCS-SC	0(0)	0(0)	2(0)	0(0)	0(0)	2(0)	0(0)
RAWS	2(1)	3(1)	2(1)	0(0)	0(0)	4(0)	0(0)
SAO	0(0)	3(0)	0(0)	1(0)	2(0)	1(0)	1(0)
SCAN	0(0)	0(0)	0(0)	1(0)	0(0)	0(0)	0(0)
SNOTEL	0(0)	0(0)	2(0)	1(0)	0(0)	0(0)	0(0)
UPR	2(0)	0(0)	0(0)	0(0)	0(0)	0(0)	0(0)
WX4U	0(0)	0(0)	0(0)	0(0)	0(0)	0(0)	0(0)
WYDOT	0(0)	0(0)	1(0)	1(0)	0(0)	0(0)	0(0)
Other	1(0)	0(0)	0(0)	1(0)	0(0)	0(0)	0(0)
Total	16(3)	40(4)	23(3)	24(2)	22(0)	34(0)	15(0)
Network	**MNRR**	**MORU**	**NIOB**	**SCBL**	**THRO**	**WICA**	
AWDN	3(0)	2(0)	4(0)	3(0)	3(0)	3(0)	
CASTNet	0(0)	1(0)	0(0)	0(0)	1(1)	1(1)	
COOP	76(3)	29(1)	12(0)	14(0)	25(1)	20(1)	
CRN	0(0)	0(0)	0(0)	0(0)	1(1)	0(0)	
CWOP	2(0)	3(0)	0(0)	2(0)	0(0)	1(0)	
GPMP	0(0)	0(0)	0(0)	0(0)	3(3)	0(0)	
GPS-MET	0(0)	0(0)	0(0)	0(0)	1(0)	0(0)	
MT DOT	0(0)	0(0)	0(0)	0(0)	0(0)	0(0)	
NADP	0(0)	1(0)	0(0)	0(0)	2(2)	1(1)	
NRCS-SC	0(0)	1(0)	0(0)	0(0)	0(0)	0(0)	
RAWS	2(0)	5(1)	0(0)	1(1)	2(0)	4(1)	
SAO	2(0)	2(0)	3(0)	1(0)	0(0)	1(0)	
SCAN	0(0)	0(0)	0(0)	0(0)	0(0)	0(0)	
SNOTEL	0(0)	1(0)	0(0)	0(0)	0(0)	0(0)	
UPR	0(0)	0(0)	0(0)	2(0)	0(0)	0(0)	
WX4U	0(0)	1(0)	0(0)	0(0)	0(0)	0(0)	
WYDOT	0(0)	0(0)	0(0)	0(0)	0(0)	0(0)	
Other	2(0)	0(0)	0(0)	1(0)	1(0)	1(0)	
Total	87(3)	46(2)	19(0)	24(1)	39(8)	32(4)	

4.2.1. South Dakota, Wyoming, and Western Nebraska

Three weather and climate stations (all active) were identified within the boundaries of AGFO (Table 4.3; Figure 4.1). The COOP station "Agate 3 E" has been active since 1900. This climate station measured only precipitation until the late 1960s. The station's data record has been very

Table 4.3. Weather and climate stations for the NGPN park units in South Dakota, Wyoming, and western Nebraska. Stations inside park units and within 40 km of the park unit boundary are included. Missing entries are indicated by "M".

Name	Lat.	Lon.	Elev. (m)	Network	Start	End	In Park?
Agate Fossil Beds National Monument (AGFO)							
Agate 3 E	42.424	-103.735	1423	COOP	4/1/1900	Present	Yes
Harrison 20 SSE	42.425	-103.736	1343	CRN	8/27/2003	Present	Yes
Agate	42.425	-103.736	1325	RAWS	7/1/1997	Present	Yes
Agate 5 N	42.508	-103.811	1447	COOP	1/1/1893	Present	No
Crawford	42.700	-103.417	1119	COOP	8/15/1984	4/1/2000	No
Crawford	42.583	-103.333	915	COOP	M	Present	No
Fort Robinson	42.667	-103.468	1158	COOP	1/1/1902	Present	No
Harrison	42.743	-103.922	1546	COOP	5/15/2003	Present	No
Harrison	42.686	-103.884	1478	COOP	3/1/1893	Present	No
Harrison 9 W	42.654	-104.047	1436	COOP	8/1/1948	Present	No
Plainsview Ranch	42.261	-103.519	1426	COOP	11/1/2002	Present	No
Torrington 29 N	42.488	-104.156	1481	COOP	4/1/1994	Present	No
Soldier Creek	42.742	-103.550	1378	RAWS	11/1/1987	7/31/1989	No
Alsop	42.334	-104.069	1327	UPR	M	Present	No
Braun	42.638	-104.099	1465	UPR	M	Present	No
Crawford	42.583	-103.333	1189	WBAN	4/1/1938	9/30/1941	No
Badlands National Park (BADL)							
Interior 3 NE	43.748	-101.941	744	COOP	11/19/1949	Present	Yes
Badlands Park HQ	43.747	-101.941	730	GPMP	10/1/1987	10/5/1992	Yes
Badlands Visitor Center	43.744	-101.941	739	GPMP	8/1/2003	Present	Yes
White River	43.511	-102.497	800	RAWS	7/1/1998	Present	Yes
Buffalo Gap	43.483	-103.317	981	AWDN	11/14/1984	6/25/1986	No
Caputa	44.000	-103.000	890	AWDN	1/1/1992	Present	No
Cottonwood	43.967	-101.867	723	AWDN	3/2/1989	Present	No
Oral	43.400	-103.267	960	AWDN	1/1/2002	Present	No
Batesland	43.217	-102.200	1041	COOP	12/16/1997	10/20/1998	No
Buffalo Gap	43.492	-103.313	972	COOP	4/1/1938	Present	No
Cottonwood 2 E	43.961	-101.861	736	COOP	6/1/1909	Present	No
Farmingdale 4 N	44.033	-102.900	961	COOP	12/1/1894	10/1/1981	No
Hermosa	43.848	-102.894	884	COOP	6/1/1998	Present	No
Hermosa 1 S	43.828	-103.196	1003	COOP	9/1/1973	Present	No
Hermosa 3 SSW	43.807	-103.213	1044	COOP	1/1/1906	Present	No
Interior	43.733	-101.983	726	COOP	11/1/1897	9/13/1979	No
Kadoka	43.835	-101.515	747	COOP	5/23/1909	Present	No
Kadoka 6 S	43.753	-101.525	647	COOP	10/14/1983	Present	No
Kyle	43.424	-102.186	875	COOP	12/1/1956	9/1/1998	No
Manderson	43.263	-102.439	943	COOP	5/1/1908	6/30/2004	No
Oglala	43.175	-102.746	913	COOP	8/1/1948	Present	No
Oral	43.403	-103.268	902	COOP	5/1/1971	Present	No
Philip	44.051	-101.601	672	COOP	11/1/1907	Present	No
Philip	44.021	-101.664	686	COOP	4/1/1985	5/1/2000	No

Name	Lat.	Lon.	Elev. (m)	Network	Start	End	In Park?
Porcupine 11 N	43.395	-102.389	860	COOP	9/1/1963	Present	No
Rockyford 5 SW	43.450	-102.567	833	COOP	6/1/1949	9/25/1956	No
Scenic	43.767	-102.550	857	COOP	7/1/1950	6/16/1981	No
Scenic	43.883	-102.447	869	COOP	10/1/1999	12/13/2002	No
The Pinnacles R.S.	43.896	-102.238	942	COOP	4/1/1978	2/13/1997	No
Wasta	44.070	-102.447	709	COOP	7/1/1925	Present	No
Wasta 3 E	44.076	-102.388	689	COOP	4/1/1988	Present	No
CW0636 Hermosa	43.898	-103.156	1052	CWOP	M	Present	No
CW5427 Hermosa	43.749	-103.244	1096	CWOP	M	Present	No
N0MN Kyle	43.420	-102.185	893	CWOP	M	Present	No
Cottonwood	43.946	-101.855	733	NADP	10/11/1983	Present	No
Pinnacles	43.882	-102.204	942	RAWS	7/1/1998	Present	No
Porcupine	43.290	-102.271	342	RAWS	6/1/1992	Present	No
Kyle	43.424	-102.186	875	SAO	12/1/1956	9/1/1998	No
Philip	44.051	-101.601	672	SAO	11/1/1907	Present	No
Philip	44.021	-101.664	686	SAO	4/1/1985	5/1/2000	No

Devils Tower National Monument (DETO)

Name	Lat.	Lon.	Elev. (m)	Network	Start	End	In Park?
Devils Tower	44.583	-104.717	1321	COOP	7/10/1932	12/31/1958	Yes
Devils Tower 2	44.583	-104.715	1177	COOP	1/1/1959	Present	Yes
Devils Tower	44.582	-104.719	1189	RAWS	1/1/1999	Present	Yes
Alva	44.700	-104.433	1219	COOP	5/1/1943	10/9/1996	No
Alva	44.652	-104.349	1338	COOP	8/1/1948	12/31/2001	No
Beulah 8 WSW	44.517	-104.267	1272	COOP	4/1/1951	7/31/1958	No
Hulett	44.686	-104.603	1145	COOP	7/1/1941	Present	No
Keyhole Dam	44.383	-104.767	1278	COOP	9/1/1949	12/31/1958	No
Knowles	44.750	-104.367	1373	COOP	1/1/1931	4/30/1943	No
Moorcroft	44.267	-104.950	1299	COOP	6/10/1976	12/19/1978	No
Moorcroft 12 NE (DCP)	44.383	-104.783	1235	COOP	12/1/1986	Present	No
Moorcroft 2	44.267	-104.933	1287	COOP	8/1/1948	11/30/1948	No
Oshoto	44.583	-104.933	1257	COOP	2/15/1926	7/18/1958	No
Oshoto 15 NW	44.783	-105.083	1220	COOP	1/1/1969	1/15/1987	No
Stroner 2 NW	44.783	-105.083	1220	COOP	4/1/1959	1/16/1969	No
Sundance	44.407	-104.374	1448	COOP	1/1/1893	10/14/2006	No
Sundance Hwy. Dept.	44.417	-104.333	1405	COOP	1/25/1984	4/2/1998	No
Bear Lodge Divide	44.550	-104.317	1426	NRCS-SC	1/1/1964	Present	No
Reuter Canyon	44.367	-104.433	1914	NRCS-SC	1/1/1965	Present	No
Bear Lodge	44.597	-104.428	1609	RAWS	1/1/1985	Present	No
Cole Canyon	44.483	-104.400	1801	SNOTEL	6/13/2000	Present	No
Warren Peak	44.400	-104.433	1987	SNOTEL	7/28/1980	Present	No
Inyan Kara I-90 W. of Sundance	44.290	-104.620	1328	WY DOT	M	Present	No

Fort Laramie National Historic Site (FOLA)

Name	Lat.	Lon.	Elev. (m)	Network	Start	End	In Park?
Ft. Laramie 1 SW DCP	42.201	-104.545	1287	COOP	11/15/1986	Present	Yes
Old Fort Laramie	42.206	-104.556	1295	COOP	1/1/1989	Present	Yes
Torrington	42.033	-104.183	1216	AWDN	9/28/1996	Present	No
Wheatland	42.083	-104.950	1416	AWDN	4/1/1985	11/23/1994	No

Name	Lat.	Lon.	Elev. (m)	Network	Start	End	In Park?
Fort Laramie 11 NNW	42.383	-104.533	1452	COOP	11/18/1927	4/15/1979	No
Guernsey 2 NW (USBR)	42.283	-104.767	1366	COOP	1/1/1992	Present	No
Guernsey Dam	42.300	-104.767	1373	COOP	9/1/1944	5/31/1962	No
Guernsey Dam No 2	42.291	-104.763	1327	COOP	5/1/1962	Present	No
Jay Em	42.467	-104.367	1406	COOP	5/1/1949	12/6/1978	No
Lingle 3 S	42.100	-104.350	1266	COOP	4/1/1952	2/15/1981	No
Torrington	42.067	-104.183	1251	COOP	5/1/1941	10/31/1948	No
Torrington 1 S	42.050	-104.183	1247	COOP	8/1/1948	7/5/1979	No
Torrington Exp. Farm	42.080	-104.224	1249	COOP	1/1/1922	Present	No
Torrington Hwy. Dept	42.083	-104.183	1251	COOP	1/25/1984	2/25/2004	No
Whalen Dam (USBR)	42.249	-104.628	1309	COOP	4/15/1949	Present	No
Wheatland 2	42.050	-104.950	1452	COOP	10/1/1934	6/30/1970	No
Wheatland 4 N	42.111	-104.949	1414	COOP	1/1/1893	Present	No
Wheatland Hwy .Dept	42.050	-104.967	1442	COOP	1/25/1984	3/29/2001	No
Yoder 2 WSW	41.913	-104.388	1320	COOP	10/1/1921	Present	No
Torrington	42.065	-104.153	1282	SAO	8/26/1999	Present	No
Torrington #1	42.070	-104.130	1305	SCAN	M	Present	No
Torrington #1	42.067	-104.133	1305	SNOTEL	M	Present	No
Torrington	42.000	-104.167	1270	WBAN	4/1/1938	8/31/1940	No
Torrington Muni.	42.070	-104.150	1282	WY DOT	M	Present	No

Jewel Cave National Monument (JECA)

Name	Lat.	Lon.	Elev. (m)	Network	Start	End	In Park?
Jewel Cave	43.717	-103.817	1681	AWDN	1/1/2002	Present	No
Wind Cave NP	43.558	-103.484	1292	CASTNet	11/1/2003	Present	No
Custer	43.774	-103.612	1670	COOP	6/22/1911	Present	No
Custer 7 SW	43.700	-103.700	1580	COOP	10/29/1948	1/15/1957	No
Deerfield 3 SE	43.994	-103.786	1847	COOP	6/1/1981	12/13/2002	No
Deerfield 4 NW	44.067	-103.900	1896	COOP	1/1/1948	6/16/1981	No
Deerfield Dam	44.017	-103.783	1790	COOP	8/1/1909	11/30/1955	No
Dewey	43.533	-104.033	1129	COOP	11/1/1948	9/30/1957	No
Dewey 15 NNE	43.717	-103.917	1552	COOP	11/1/1948	6/30/1958	No
Dewey 8 ENE	43.550	-103.900	1241	COOP	11/1/1948	11/30/1967	No
Edgemont 10 N	43.450	-103.833	1202	COOP	11/1/1948	9/30/1957	No
Edgemont 23 NNW	43.624	-103.917	1342	COOP	11/1/1967	Present	No
Hill City	43.938	-103.571	1518	COOP	4/1/1909	Present	No
Hot Springs 7 W	43.433	-103.600	1214	COOP	11/1/1948	6/30/1958	No
Keystone	43.904	-103.410	1352	COOP	7/24/1990	10/1/1997	No
Medicine Mountain	43.904	-103.726	1847	COOP	12/1/1997	Present	No
Moon	43.950	-104.000	1937	COOP	11/1/1949	10/27/1957	No
Mount Coolidge	43.750	-103.483	1951	COOP	9/1/1952	12/31/1974	No
Mountain Meadow	44.005	-103.832	1836	COOP	2/26/2002	Present	No
Mt. Rushmore Natl. Mem.	43.877	-103.458	1600	COOP	2/1/1962	Present	No
Newcastle	43.858	-104.214	1315	COOP	7/1/1906	Present	No
Newcastle 15 SSE	43.667	-104.133	1208	COOP	9/1/1948	7/31/1958	No
Newcastle Hwy. Dept.	43.833	-104.200	1321	COOP	1/25/1984	5/28/1998	No
Redfern	44.000	-103.650	1681	COOP	8/1/1951	6/30/1955	No
Wind Cave	43.561	-103.488	1262	COOP	8/1/1948	Present	No

Name	Lat.	Lon.	Elev. (m)	Network	Start	End	In Park?
Newcastle	43.873	-104.192	1466	NADP	8/11/1981	Present	No
Wind Cave NP-Elk Mountain	43.558	-103.484	1311	NADP	11/5/2002	Present	No
Ditch Creek	43.867	-103.783	2100	NRCS-SC	1/1/1989	Present	No
Little Bear Run	43.967	-104.050	1903	NRCS-SC	1/1/1992	Present	No
Custer	43.750	-103.633	1585	RAWS	5/1/2000	Present	No
Mt. Rushmore	43.875	-103.458	1646	RAWS	10/1/2000	Present	No
Red Canyon	43.426	-103.759	1415	RAWS	5/1/1993	Present	No
WICA-Elk Mountain	43.561	-103.491	1253	RAWS	6/1/1996	Present	No
Custer	43.733	-103.611	1690	SAO	1/19/1983	Present	No
Mount Rushmore National Memorial (MORU)							
Mt. Rushmore Natl. Mem.	43.877	-103.458	1600	COOP	2/1/1962	Present	Yes
Mt. Rushmore	43.875	-103.458	1646	RAWS	10/1/2000	Present	Yes
Caputa	44.000	-103.000	890	AWDN	1/1/1992	Present	No
Jewel Cave	43.717	-103.817	1681	AWDN	1/1/2002	Present	No
Wind Cave NP	43.558	-103.484	1292	CASTNet	11/1/2003	Present	No
Camp Columbus	44.133	-103.433	1296	COOP	M	Present	No
Custer	43.774	-103.612	1670	COOP	6/22/1911	Present	No
Custer 7 SW	43.700	-103.700	1580	COOP	10/29/1948	1/15/1957	No
Custer Crossing Camp	44.206	-103.649	1646	COOP	11/1/1999	Present	No
Deerfield 3 SE	43.994	-103.786	1847	COOP	6/1/1981	12/13/2002	No
Deerfield Dam	44.017	-103.783	1790	COOP	8/1/1909	11/30/1955	No
Hermosa 1 S	43.828	-103.196	1003	COOP	9/1/1973	Present	No
Hermosa 3 SSW	43.807	-103.213	1044	COOP	1/1/1906	Present	No
Hill City	43.938	-103.571	1518	COOP	4/1/1909	Present	No
Johnson Siding	44.084	-103.438	1311	COOP	8/1/1973	Present	No
Keystone	43.904	-103.410	1352	COOP	7/24/1990	10/1/1997	No
Medicine Mountain	43.904	-103.726	1847	COOP	12/1/1997	Present	No
Mount Coolidge	43.750	-103.483	1951	COOP	9/1/1952	12/31/1974	No
Mountain Meadow	44.005	-103.832	1836	COOP	2/26/2002	Present	No
Mystic	44.083	-103.650	1470	COOP	8/1/1951	6/30/1958	No
Nemo 5 SE	44.150	-103.450	1316	COOP	1/1/1980	2/20/2001	No
Pactola Dam	44.062	-103.482	1439	COOP	7/1/1951	Present	No
Rapid City	44.043	-103.054	963	COOP	1/1/1949	Present	No
Rapid City	44.115	-103.283	1052	COOP	4/11/1972	Present	No
Rapid City	44.073	-103.211	1030	COOP	1/1/1996	Present	No
Rapid City	44.067	-103.200	988	COOP	1/1/1888	4/11/1972	No
Rapid City 2	44.086	-103.242	985	COOP	1/1/1980	Present	No
Rapid City No. 3	44.053	-103.311	M	COOP	10/1/1984	Present	No
Redfern	44.000	-103.650	1681	COOP	8/1/1951	6/30/1955	No
Rochford	44.133	-103.717	1613	COOP	5/1/1948	2/28/1951	No
Rochford 2 WNW	44.132	-103.751	1661	COOP	10/1/1897	Present	No
Rushmore Cave	43.872	-103.338	1155	COOP	9/1/1973	6/1/2000	No
Wind Cave	43.561	-103.488	1262	COOP	8/1/1948	Present	No
CW0636 Hermosa	43.898	-103.156	1052	CWOP	M	Present	No
CW1874 Box Elder	44.100	-103.067	966	CWOP	M	Present	No

Name	Lat.	Lon.	Elev. (m)	Network	Start	End	In Park?
CW5427 Hermosa	43.749	-103.244	1096	CWOP	M	Present	No
Wind Cave NP-Elk Mountain	43.558	-103.484	1311	NADP	11/5/2002	Present	No
Ditch Creek	43.867	-103.783	2100	NRCS-SC	1/1/1989	Present	No
Baker Park	43.979	-103.425	1425	RAWS	10/1/2001	Present	No
Custer	43.750	-103.633	1585	RAWS	5/1/2000	Present	No
Nemo	44.192	-103.510	1415	RAWS	5/1/1993	Present	No
WICA-Elk Mountain	43.561	-103.491	1253	RAWS	6/1/1996	Present	No
Custer	43.733	-103.611	1690	SAO	1/19/1983	Present	No
Rapid City	44.043	-103.054	963	SAO	1/1/1949	Present	No
Maitland Draw	44.117	-103.800	1798	SNOTEL	M	Present	No
Terricita Hills Rapid City	44.045	-103.233	1052	WX4U	M	Present	No
Scotts Bluff National Monument (SCBL)							
Scotts Bluff	41.817	-103.700	1287	RAWS	8/1/2001	Present	Yes
Mitchell Farms	41.933	-103.700	1098	AWDN	7/11/1996	Present	No
Panhandle	41.933	-103.700	1244	AWDN	8/21/1982	9/22/1992	No
Scottsbluff	41.883	-103.667	1208	AWDN	1/1/1991	Present	No
Bayard	41.815	-103.290	1179	COOP	11/1/2001	Present	No
Gering	41.834	-103.678	1205	COOP	10/1/1998	Present	No
Gering 2 W	41.817	-103.683	1254	COOP	8/1/1948	11/30/1949	No
Harrisburg 12 WNW	41.633	-103.954	1387	COOP	7/1/1911	Present	No
Henry	41.989	-104.053	1226	COOP	8/1/1978	Present	No
Henry 6 N	42.083	-104.033	1281	COOP	7/1/1921	9/30/1953	No
Lyman	41.917	-104.036	1234	COOP	12/23/1924	Present	No
Minatare 2 S	41.783	-103.517	1162	COOP	6/1/1972	6/9/1994	No
Minatare Dam	41.918	-103.484	1263	COOP	1/1/1925	Present	No
Mitchell	41.948	-103.701	1244	COOP	6/1/1909	Present	No
Mitchell 1 S	41.933	-103.800	1198	COOP	5/1/1972	12/23/1994	No
Scottsbluff	41.864	-103.640	1191	COOP	1/1/1998	Present	No
Scottsbluff	42.031	-103.702	1294	COOP	10/1/2002	9/1/2005	No
Scottsbluff	41.871	-103.593	1202	COOP	1/1/1893	Present	No
CW4928 Scottsbluff	41.867	-103.667	1185	CWOP	M	Present	No
KC4WTI Gering	41.815	-103.673	1193	CWOP	M	Present	No
Scottsbluff	41.871	-103.593	1202	SAO	1/1/1893	Present	No
Joyce	41.944	-103.979	1253	UPR	M	Present	No
Melba	41.767	-103.472	1162	UPR	M	Present	No
Scottsbluff	41.867	-103.583	1207	WBAN	1/1/1943	9/30/1944	No
Wind Cave National Park (WICA)							
Wind Cave NP	43.558	-103.484	1292	CASTNet	11/1/2003	Present	Yes
Wind Cave	43.561	-103.488	1262	COOP	8/1/1948	Present	Yes
Wind Cave NP-Elk Mountain	43.558	-103.484	1311	NADP	11/5/2002	Present	Yes
WICA-Elk Mountain	43.561	-103.491	1253	RAWS	6/1/1996	Present	Yes
Buffalo Gap	43.483	-103.317	981	AWDN	11/14/1984	6/25/1986	No
Jewel Cave	43.717	-103.817	1681	AWDN	1/1/2002	Present	No
Oral	43.400	-103.267	960	AWDN	1/1/2002	Present	No

Name	Lat.	Lon.	Elev. (m)	Network	Start	End	In Park?
Angostura Dam	43.350	-103.433	958	COOP	10/1/1947	5/13/1971	No
Buffalo Gap	43.492	-103.313	972	COOP	4/1/1938	Present	No
Custer	43.774	-103.612	1670	COOP	6/22/1911	Present	No
Custer 7 SW	43.700	-103.700	1580	COOP	10/29/1948	1/15/1957	No
Dewey 8 ENE	43.550	-103.900	1241	COOP	11/1/1948	11/30/1967	No
Edgemont 10 N	43.450	-103.833	1202	COOP	11/1/1948	9/30/1957	No
Edgemont 23 NNW	43.624	-103.917	1342	COOP	11/1/1967	Present	No
Hermosa 1 S	43.828	-103.196	1003	COOP	9/1/1973	Present	No
Hermosa 3 SSW	43.807	-103.213	1044	COOP	1/1/1906	Present	No
Hot Springs	43.438	-103.474	1085	COOP	2/1/1894	Present	No
Hot Springs 7 W	43.433	-103.600	1214	COOP	11/1/1948	6/30/1958	No
Hot Springs 9 SW	43.300	-103.550	1000	COOP	11/1/1948	9/30/1957	No
Hot Springs Fall R.	43.431	-103.477	1040	COOP	11/1/1988	Present	No
Keystone	43.904	-103.410	1352	COOP	7/24/1990	10/1/1997	No
Mount Coolidge	43.750	-103.483	1951	COOP	9/1/1952	12/31/1974	No
Mt. Rushmore Natl. Mem.	43.877	-103.458	1600	COOP	2/1/1962	Present	No
Oral	43.403	-103.268	902	COOP	5/1/1971	Present	No
Rushmore Cave	43.872	-103.338	1155	COOP	9/1/1973	6/1/2000	No
Smithwick 6 SW	43.267	-103.317	976	COOP	11/1/1948	9/30/1957	No
CW5427 Hermosa	43.749	-103.244	1096	CWOP	M	Present	No
Custer	43.750	-103.633	1585	RAWS	5/1/2000	Present	No
Mt. Rushmore	43.875	-103.458	1646	RAWS	10/1/2000	Present	No
Red Canyon	43.426	-103.759	1415	RAWS	5/1/1993	Present	No
Custer	43.733	-103.611	1690	SAO	1/19/1983	Present	No
Hot Springs	43.367	-103.383	960	WBAN	4/1/1952	12/31/1960	No

complete since 1980. The CRN station "Harrison 20 SSE" is a valuable near-real-time station that has been active since 2003 and should provide a useful long-term climate record in the future. Another near-real-time station within AGFO is the RAWS weather station "Agate," which has been active since 1997. A large gap occurred at this RAWS site from October to December of 1998 but the data record has been complete since that time.

Nine COOP stations were identified within 40 km of AGFO (Table 4.3). All but one of these stations are active. The COOP station "Agate 5 N" is closest to AGFO, located 8 km north of the park unit. This COOP station also provides the longest data record of the stations we identified for AGFO, having been active since January 1893. Unfortunately, the reliability of the data record at "Agate 5 N" is uncertain. A more reliable record is found at the COOP station "Harrison," which is 29 km northwest of AGFO and only has a few data gaps, the most recent being in November 2006. This climate station has been active since March 1893. The COOP station "Fort Robinson" is 34 km northeast of AGFO and has been active since 1902. The data record at this COOP station was very complete until 1970. Numerous data gaps occurred at "Fort Robinson" in the 1970s and early 1980s. No observations were available from the late 1980s until February 2006. After February 2006, the data record has been more complete but no weekend observations have been taken. The COOP station "Harrison 9 W" is 32 km northwest of

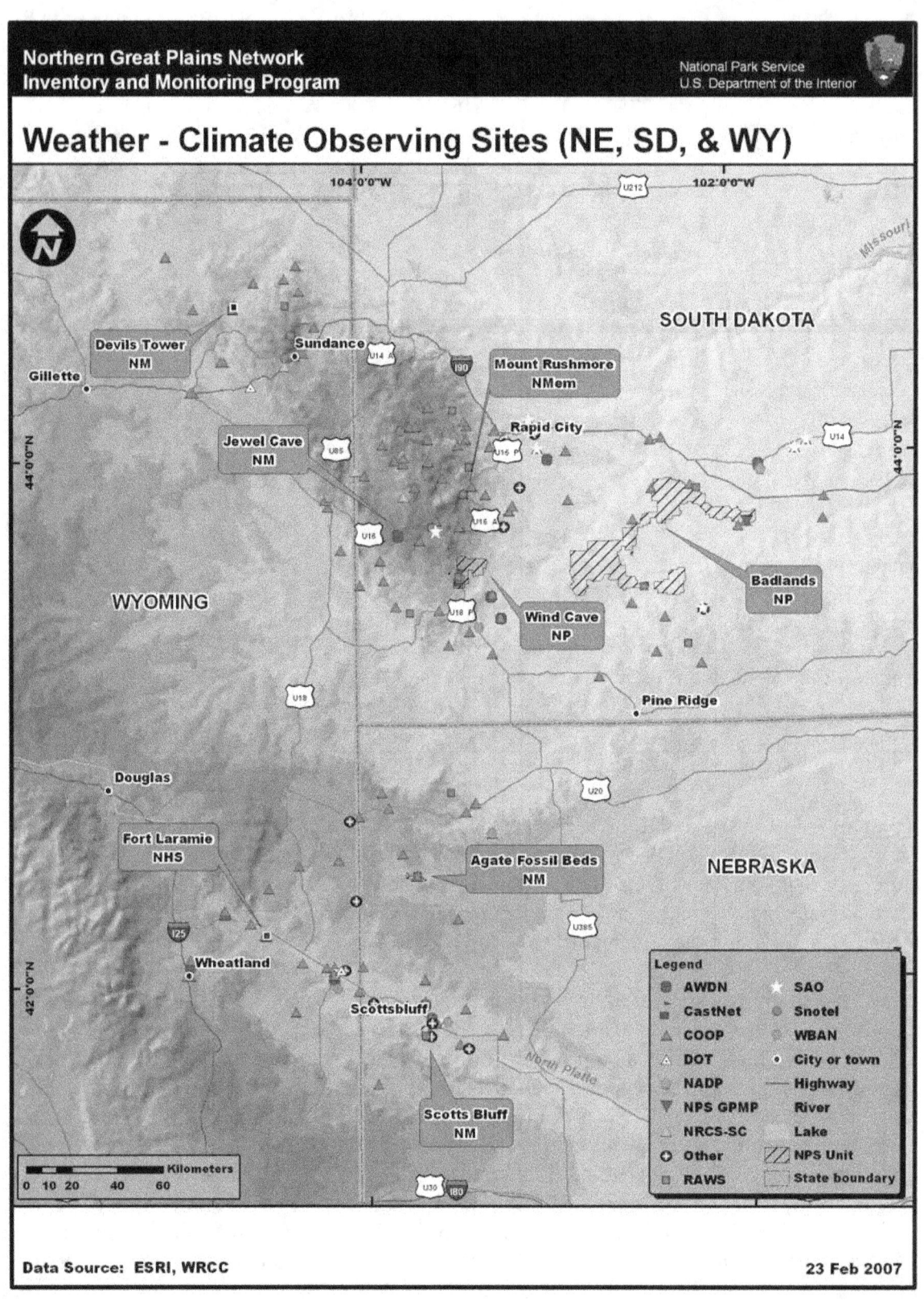

Figure 4.1. Station locations for the NGPN park units in South Dakota, Wyoming, and western Nebraska.

AGFO and has a data record going back to 1948. Unfortunately, the data record at this COOP station is very incomplete. The RAWS station "Soldier Creek" operated from 1987-1989, about 37 km northeast of AGFO. The only other sources of near-real-time weather data we identified besides the RAWS station inside AGFO (Agate) are two UPR stations, one in Alsop and the other in Braun. Both of these stations are west of AGFO, near the Nebraska/Wyoming border.

We identified four stations (three active) within BADL (Table 4.3; Figure 4.1). The COOP station "Interior 3 NE," located in the northeastern corner of BADL, is the primary climate record within the park unit, with data going back to 1949. This data record has been largely complete since 1955, with scattered small gaps. The last significant data gap occurred in June 2006. A GPMP station has operating at the main BADL visitor center since 2003. The primary source of near-real-time data in BADL is the RAWS station "White River," which is located in southern BADL and has been active since 1998. A large data gap occurred at this site from November 1998 to June 1999 but the data record has been complete since that time.

We identified four AWDN stations (three active) within 40 km of BADL (Table 4.3). "Cottonwood" is located northeast of BADL, while the remaining AWDN stations are located to the west of BADL (Figure 4.1).

Out of the 23 COOP stations we identified within 40 km of the boundaries of BADL, 13 are active (Table 4.3). The longest record we identified was from the COOP station "Hermosa 3 SSW," which is 31 km northwest of BADL and has been active since 1906. This site measures precipitation only. Numerous data gaps exist in this record; most of these gaps occurred before 1960s and during the 1970s and 1980s. The record has been very reliable since 1990. The COOP station "Philip" is 37 km northeast of BADL and has been active since 1907. The reliability of the data record at "Philip" is uncertain, as there are numerous, large data gaps throughout the record. The COOP station "Kadoka" is 31 km east of BADL and has been active since 1909. The data record at "Kadoka" had a large gap from March 1978 through November 1998, but has been very reliable since that time. The COOP station "Wasta" (1925-present) is 16 km north of BADL and has a data record which was very reliable up until 2002. Only one active SAO station, "Philip," was identified for BADL (Table 4.3). This station is collocated with the COOP station "Philip."

One NADP station and two RAWS stations currently operate within 40 km of BADL (Table 4.3). The NADP station "Cottonwood" is 17 km northeast of BADL and has been operating since 1983. The RAWS stations "Pinnacles" and "Porcupine" both have reliable data records. "Pinnacles" is less than a kilometer from the northern edge of BADL (Figure 4.1) and has been active since 1998. "Porcupine" is 21 km south of BADL and has been active since 1992.

We identified three stations (two active) within DETO (Table 4.3). The COOP station "Devils Tower 2" (1959-present) has a very reliable data record. The primary source of near-real-time data in DETO is the RAWS station "Devils Tower," which has been active since 1999. A large data gap occurred at this site from March to July of 2003.

We identified 14 COOP stations within 40 km of the boundaries of DETO; however, only two of these stations are still active (Table 4.3). The COOP station "Hulett" is 12 km northeast of

DETO and has been operating since 1941. The data record at this site has a significant gap from December 1975 to June 1991. The other active COOP station we identified, "Moorcroft 12 NE (DCP)," is 22 km south of DETO. This station, which has been active since 1986, has numerous data gaps.

The primary sources of near-real-time weather data outside of DETO come from sites to the southeast of the park unit (Figure 4.1). The RAWS station "Bear Lodge" is 22 km east of DETO and has been active since 1985 (Table 4.3). Data gaps occurred at "Bear Lodge" from May 1987 to October 1988 and in December 1988. Two NRCS-SC sites and two SNOTEL sites were identified in the hills around Sundance, Wyoming, to the south and east of DETO. The two NRCS-SC sites we identified ("Bear Lodge Divide" and "Reuter Canyon") have been taking manual snow measurements since the mid-1960s. The SNOTEL station "Cole Canyon" is 26 km southeast of DETO and has been operating since 2000. The SNOTEL station "Warren Peak" is 29 km southeast of DETO and has been operating since 1980.

We identified two stations within FOLA (Table 4.3). The COOP station "Fort Laramie 1 SW DCP" (1986-present) has a data record of doubtful reliability, while the data record from the COOP station "Old Fort Laramie" (1989-present) has been very reliable.

We identified two AWDN stations (one active) within 40 km of FOLA (Table 4.3). The active AWDN station, "Torrington," is 34 km southeast of FOLA (Figure 4.1) and has been operating since 1996. The other sources of near-real-time weather data for FOLA are also located in the Torrington area, southeast of FOLA. The SAO station "Torrington" has been operating since 1999. Both a SCAN and a SNOTEL site operate in this area as well.

Out of the 15 COOP stations we identified within 40 km of the boundaries of FOLA, six are active (Table 4.3). The longest record we identified was from the COOP station "Wheatland 4 N," which is 33 km southwest of FOLA and has been active since 1893. Numerous data gaps occurred at this station in the 1910s and 1920s, but the data record has been very reliable since that time. The COOP station "Torrington Exp. Farm" is 28 km southeast of FOLA and has a very reliable data record extending back to 1922. The COOP station "Yoder 2 WSW" is 34 km southeast of FOLA and has a data record (1921-present) that is largely complete, with scattered small data gaps throughout its record. The COOP station "Whalen Dam (USBR)" (1949-present) is 7 km west of FOLA and has a data record which was very reliable up until 1991.

No weather or climate stations were identified within the boundaries of JECA (Table 4.3). An AWDN station (Jewel Cave; 2002-present) is located just outside the park unit. The CASTNet station at WICA (discussed below) is 32 km southeast of JECA (Figure 4.1). Four RAWS stations (all active) were identified within 40 km of JECA. The closest of these is "Custer," 15 km east of JECA, which has a complete data record going back to 2000. The longest record comes from the RAWS station "Red Canyon," which is 33 km south of JECA; this site has been operating since 1993. The RAWS station at Mount Rushmore (discussed below) is 32 km northeast of JECA. The only RAWS station with notable data gaps is "WICA-Elk Mountain," 32 km southeast of JECA, which had no observations from April to June of 1998.

Of the 23 COOP stations identified within 40 km of JECA, seven are active (Table 4.3). The closest active COOP station to JECA is "Edgemont 23 NNW" (1967-present), located 12 km southwest of the park unit. The COOP station "Newcastle" provides the longest data record we identified among these active COOP stations, going back to 1906. This data record is largely complete, with scattered data gaps. The data record at the COOP station "Hill City" (1909-present), 30 km northeast of JECA, is of unknown reliability until 1954. This site measured only precipitation until 1968, when sporadic temperature observations began and continued through the 1970s. This station's record has only been complete for both precipitation and temperature since 1988. "Custer" is another long-term COOP station (1911-present) that we identified for JECA. This station is 17 km northeast of JECA and has a data record that is largely complete, with scattered gaps. The COOP station "Wind Cave" (1948-present), discussed below, is 32 km southeast of JECA.

Two stations have been identified within MORU (Table 4.3). The COOP station "Mount Rushmore Natl. Mem." has been active since 1962 and has a very reliable climate record. The only gap we noted for this station occurred in October 2003. The RAWS station "Mt. Rushmore" is the primary source of near-real-time weather data in MORU. This station has a very reliable data record going back to 2000.

We identified 28 COOP stations within 40 km of the boundaries of MORU. Seventeen of these are active (Table 4.3). The longest record we identified was from the COOP station "Rochford 2 WNW," which is 35 km northwest of MORU and has been active since 1897. The data record at this station has not been reliable, with numerous, large data gaps throughout its record. The COOP station "Hermosa 3 SSW," discussed previously, is 20 km southeast of MORU. The COOP station "Hill City," discussed previously, is 10 km northwest of MORU. "Rapid City" (1949-present), 35 km northeast of MORU at the Rapid City Regional Airport, has a fairly complete data record, with scattered data gaps. The COOP station "Wind Cave," discussed below, is 34 km south of MORU.

A handful of weather networks provide near-real-time data within 40 km of MORU. The AWDN network has two active stations in this region; "Caputa" is 37 km northeast of MORU while "Jewel Cave" is 33 km southwest of MORU. The CASTNet station at WICA, discussed below, is 35 km south of MORU. Four RAWS stations are located within 40 km of MORU. "Custer," discussed previously, is 19 km southwest of MORU. "WICA-Elk Mountain," discussed previously, is 34 km south of MORU. "Baker Park," 10 km north of MORU, has been active since 2001 and has a reliable data record. Another reliable data record is found at "Nemo," which is 34 km north of MORU and has been active since 1993. The two SAO stations we identified are in Custer, 19 km southwest of MORU, and at the Rapid City Regional Airport, 35 km northeast of MORU. The SNOTEL station "Maitland Draw" is 37 km northwest of MORU. In addition to these stations, several CWOP and WX4U stations also provide near-real-time data within 40 km of MORU.

One weather/climate stations was identified within SCBL (Table 4.3). The RAWS station "Scotts Bluff" has been active since 2001 and has a very reliable data record. Prior to the installation of this RAWS site, a manual weather station was operated by SCBL staff at the same location, with written records of daily precipitation and maximum and minimum temperatures going back to at least July 1984.

We identified three AWDN stations (two active) within 40 km of SCBL (Table 4.3). The AWDN station "Mitchell Farms" is 9 km north of SCBL (Figure 4.1) and has been operating since 1996. The AWDN station "Scottsbluff" is 4 km northeast of SCBL and has been operating since 1991. The other sources of near-real-time weather data for SCBL are also located primarily in the Scottsbluff area, northeast of SCBL, including two CWOP stations and one SAO station at Western Nebraska Regional Airport. The UPR network has two stations within 40 km of SCBL.

We identified 14 COOP stations within 40 km of the boundaries of SCBL. Nine of these are active (Table 4.3). The longest record we identified was from the COOP station "Scottsbluff," which is 8 km northeast of SCBL and has been active since 1893. The data record at this station is quite reliable. The COOP station "Mitchell" (1909-present) is 10 km northwest of SCBL. The data record at "Mitchell" has scattered data gaps throughout, including a large gap from May 1999 to December 2001. The COOP station "Harrisburg 12 WNW," active since 1911, is 28 km southwest of SCBL. This station measured only precipitation until 1961, after which temperature observations have been included. The data record at this station is very reliable. The COOP station "Lyman" (1924-present), 27 km west of SCBL, measures precipitation only and has a very reliable data record. The COOP station "Minatare Dam" (1925-present) is 18 km northeast of SCBL but has an unreliable data record.

Four weather and climate stations were identified within WICA (Table 4.3). The CASTNet station "Wind Cave NP" has been operating since 2003 and provides near-real-time data for the park unit. The RAWS station "WICA-Elk Mountain," discussed previously, provides another source of near-real-time data for the park unit. The main source for long-term climate data in WICA is the COOP station "Wind Cave," which has provided data since 1948. This climate station has had a complete data record since August 1990. Before 1990, this data record was of doubtful reliability. A NADP site (Wind Cave NP-Elk Mountain) has been operating in WICA since 2002.

We identified three AWDN stations (two active) within 40 km of WICA (Table 4.3). The AWDN stations "Jewel Cave" and "Oral" both started taking measurements in 2002. "Jewel Cave" is 27 km northwest of WICA while "Oral" is 20 km southeast of WICA (Figure 4.1).

Three other weather networks provide sources of near-real-time weather data for WICA. One CWOP station is located in Hermosa, about 30 km northeast of WICA. The SAO station at Custer is 14 km northwest of WICA. Finally, three active RAWS sites, all of which have been discussed previously, are located within 40 km of WICA. "Custer" is 17 km northwest of WICA, "Mt. Rushmore" is 26 km north of WICA, and "Red Canyon" is 22 km southwest of WICA.

Nineteen COOP stations were identified within 40 km of the boundaries of WICA. Nine of these are active (Table 4.3). The longest record we identified was from the COOP station "Hot Springs," 9 km south of WICA; this climate station has been active since 1894. The data record at this station is very reliable. The COOP station "Hermosa 3 SSW," discussed previously, is 23 km northeast of WICA. The COOP station "Custer," discussed previously, is 18 km northwest of

WICA. The COOP station "Buffalo Gap," active since 1938, is 9 km southeast of WICA. This climate station measured only precipitation until 2000. A large data gap occurred at "Buffalo Gap" from May 2000 to April 2004. Both temperature and precipitation have been measured at this site since April 2004.

4.2.2. North Dakota

No weather or climate stations were identified within FOUS (Table 4.4). Three AWDN stations are located within 40 km of the park unit. "Brorson," 28 km southwest of FOUS (Figure 4.2), has been active since 1995. "Sidney," 30 km southwest of FOUS, has also been active since 1995. The longest active AWDN station is "Williston," 26 km northeast of FOUS. The MT DOT and SAO networks are the other main sources of near-real-time data for FOUS. The MT DOT station along U.S. Highway 2 near the Montana/North Dakota border is the closest active station to FOUS, 14 km north of the park unit. Active SAO stations are located in both Sydney and Williston, with both stations having data records that are over 40 years in length.

Table 4.4. Weather and climate stations for NGPN park units in North Dakota. Stations inside park units and within 40 km of the park unit boundary are included. Missing entries are indicated by "M".

Name	Lat.	Lon.	Elev. (m)	Network	Start	End	In Park?
Fort Union Trading Post National Historic Site (FOUS)							
Brorson	47.783	-104.250	691	AWDN	1/1/1995	Present	No
Sidney	47.733	-104.150	585	AWDN	1/1/1995	Present	No
Williston	48.133	-103.733	640	AWDN	3/21/1989	Present	No
Alexander 18 SW	47.700	-103.983	620	COOP	10/1/1963	4/1/1985	No
Alexander 4 NNW	47.902	-103.661	652	COOP	6/1/1916	Present	No
Bainville 6 NE	48.183	-104.126	654	COOP	7/1/2006	Present	No
Culbertson	48.150	-104.509	592	COOP	12/1/1900	Present	No
Culbertson 3 SE	48.123	-104.476	574	COOP	7/1/1972	Present	No
Culbertson 6 NE	48.217	-104.433	641	COOP	7/1/1948	9/30/1951	No
Culbertson SCS Office	48.150	-104.517	586	COOP	7/1/1948	9/30/1951	No
Fairview	47.850	-104.050	589	COOP	10/1/1932	5/31/1956	No
Nohly 4 NW	48.033	-104.133	580	COOP	1/1/1951	10/31/1981	No
Sidney	47.728	-104.147	589	COOP	10/16/1910	Present	No
Sidney 2 S	47.678	-104.156	573	COOP	1/1/1956	Present	No
Williston	48.174	-103.637	580	COOP	1/1/1962	Present	No
Williston	48.150	-103.617	578	COOP	11/1/1893	1/19/1962	No
Williston 5 SW	48.108	-103.714	558	COOP	11/1/1908	Present	No
Williston Exp. Farm	48.138	-103.737	642	COOP	7/1/1956	Present	No
Sioux Pass MT-16 MP 21	47.920	-104.326	756	MT DOT	M	Present	No
US-2 @Stateline US2 MP 667.1	48.138	-104.047	640	MT DOT	M	Present	No
Sidney	47.717	-104.183	604	SAO	9/1/1954	Present	No
Williston	48.174	-103.637	580	SAO	1/1/1962	Present	No
Knife River Indian Villages National Historic Site (KNRI)							
Hazen	47.300	-101.683	552	AWDN	6/29/1993	Present	No
Beulah 1 W	47.262	-101.791	544	COOP	5/1/1916	Present	No
Center	47.064	-101.212	607	COOP	4/1/1938	Present	No

Name	Lat.	Lon.	Elev. (m)	Network	Start	End	In Park?
Garrison 1 NNW	47.651	-101.417	590	COOP	1/1/1937	Present	No
Hazen 1 S	47.294	-101.629	522	COOP	7/1/1972	1/11/2005	No
Riverdale	47.498	-101.375	603	COOP	9/1/1948	Present	No
Stanton	47.317	-101.383	519	COOP	8/1/1923	4/30/1936	No
Underwood	47.455	-101.146	623	COOP	4/25/1952	Present	No
Underwood 12 W	47.433	-101.400	534	COOP	2/1/1912	4/30/1952	No
Washburn	47.284	-101.027	529	COOP	8/1/1893	Present	No
Washburn Power Plant	47.283	-101.033	503	COOP	3/17/1921	12/31/1969	No
Washburn River	47.289	-101.036	500	COOP	7/1/1973	9/28/2005	No
Washburn Water Works	47.283	-101.033	528	COOP	6/1/1950	11/30/1959	No
W0BIS-6 Center	47.107	-101.290	607	CWOP	M	Present	No
Garrison	47.646	-101.439	582	SAO	7/16/1991	Present	No
Theodore Roosevelt National Park (THRO)							
Painted Canyon	46.895	-103.378	850	CASTNet	8/1/1998	Present	Yes
Watford City 14 S	47.600	-103.260	618	COOP	6/1/1951	Present	Yes
Medora 7 E	46.895	-103.377	850	CRN	9/18/2004	Present	Yes
Painted Canyon	46.895	-103.378	850	GPMP	7/1/1998	Present	Yes
Theodore Roosevelt N	47.601	-103.264	624	GPMP	2/1/1980	12/1/1997	Yes
Theodore Roosevelt S	47.601	-103.264	624	GPMP	1/1/1980	12/31/1989	Yes
Theodore Roosevelt NP	47.601	-103.264	611	NADP	5/5/1981	12/12/2000	Yes
Theodore Roosevelt NP	46.895	-103.378	841	NADP	1/30/2001	Present	Yes
Beach	46.783	-103.967	884	AWDN	6/29/1993	Present	No
Dickinson	46.900	-102.817	760	AWDN	1/1/1990	Present	No
Watford City	47.800	-103.283	676	AWDN	1/1/1993	Present	No
Alexander 4 NNW	47.902	-103.661	652	COOP	6/1/1916	Present	No
Beach	46.913	-104.007	850	COOP	8/1/1906	Present	No
Belfield 1 SW	46.883	-103.183	793	COOP	1/1/1948	7/12/1978	No
Bowman 30 NNW	46.583	-103.517	766	COOP	3/1/1951	6/30/1958	No
Dickinson Exp. Stn.	46.891	-102.811	750	COOP	1/1/1893	Present	No
Fairfield	47.191	-103.225	838	COOP	8/1/1928	Present	No
Fryburg 1 SSE	46.867	-103.300	833	COOP	4/1/1918	7/1/1958	No
Golva 1 SE	46.733	-103.950	848	COOP	1/1/1948	10/31/1952	No
Grassy Butte	47.400	-103.233	811	COOP	5/1/1950	11/30/1961	No
Grassy Butte 10 N	47.517	-103.233	763	COOP	3/16/1950	9/30/1957	No
Grassy Butte 2 ENE	47.401	-103.207	814	COOP	6/24/1987	Present	No
Keene 3 S	47.897	-102.921	753	COOP	8/2/1950	Present	No
Killdeer 8 NW	47.467	-102.833	578	COOP	4/1/1893	11/30/1996	No
Medora	46.916	-103.526	691	COOP	7/1/1948	Present	No
Medora	46.917	-103.517	692	COOP	1/1/1893	9/30/1955	No
Medora 22 NNW	47.233	-103.600	689	COOP	8/1/1951	10/2/1973	No
Medora State Park	46.917	-103.550	692	COOP	1/1/1948	12/31/1949	No
New Hradec 1 E	47.000	-102.867	M	COOP	M	Present	No
Searing	47.567	-103.800	M	COOP	8/16/1948	12/31/1949	No
Sentinel Butte 20 S	46.617	-103.817	811	COOP	1/1/1948	1/1/1976	No
Trotters	47.284	-103.901	738	COOP	12/1/1949	Present	No
Trotters 6 SE	47.300	-103.867	741	COOP	1/1/1926	7/31/1959	No

Name	Lat.	Lon.	Elev. (m)	Network	Start	End	In Park?
Watford City	47.804	-103.289	661	COOP	1/1/1912	Present	No
Watford City 12 E	47.800	-102.983	640	COOP	8/1/1950	10/31/1995	No
Medora	46.910	-103.270	839	GPS-MET	M	Present	No
Sand Creek	46.546	-103.518	823	RAWS	8/1/1997	Present	No
Watford City	47.780	-103.287	660	RAWS	7/1/1997	Present	No
Golva	46.733	-103.950	849	WBAN	3/1/1935	12/31/1946	No

Fifteen COOP stations have been identified within 40 km of the boundaries of FOUS. Nine of these are still active (Table 4.4). The closest active COOP station to FOUS is "Bainville 6 NE" (2006-present), which is 21 km north of FOUS. The COOP station "Nohly 4 NW" was closer (7 km northwest of FOUS), but this station is no longer active (1951-1981). The longest record we identified was from the COOP station "Culbertson," which has been taking measurements since 1900. This climate station is 38 km northwest of FOUS. The data record at this station is largely complete. However, a longer record may be available from Williston. Two COOP stations have been identified as "Williston." One of these stations operated from November 1893 until January 1962. The second "Williston" station has been active since January 1962. These start and end dates indicate that these two records may actually be from the same station, providing a data record from 1893 until the present. The differing latitude/longitude coordinates between these two sites indicate that a station move may have occurred during 1962. Therefore, these records should be interpreted with caution. The COOP station "Williston 5 SW," 36 km east of FOUS, has been active since 1908 and measures only precipitation. Unfortunately, the data record at this station has been very unreliable. The COOP station "Sidney" has been active since 1910. This climate station is 21 km southwest of FOUS and with the exception of a large gap from October 1922 to March 1949, has a very reliable data record. The COOP station "Alexander 4 NNW" is 29 km east of FOUS. This climate station has been operating since 1916 and measures only precipitation. Unfortunately, the data record at this station has numerous data gaps.

No weather or climate stations were identified within KNRI (Table 4.4). Out of the 12 COOP stations identified within 40 km of the boundaries of KNRI, six are still active. The closest COOP station to KNRI is "Riverdale," 12 km west of the park unit. This climate station's data record goes back to 1948 and was reliable until the late 1970s. The station produced very unreliable data during the 1980s and 1990s. Since 2000, measurements have commenced, but usually without weekend observations. Weekend observations have only recently been resumed at "Riverdale." The longest record we identified was from the COOP station "Washburn" (1893-present), which is 26 km east of KNRI. This station had a large gap in its record from October 1993 to April 1996, with scattered data gaps elsewhere in the record. A reliable long-term record was identified at the COOP station "Beulah 1 W," which is 32 km west of KNRI and has been active since 1916. The COOP station "Center" (1938-present) also has a very reliable record. This station is 31 km south of KNRI. The COOP station "Garrison 1 NNW," which is 29 km north of KNRI, has been active since 1937 and has scattered, small data gaps.

The AWDN and SAO networks are the two primary sources of automated weather data for KNRI. The AWDN station "Hazen" is 22 km west of KNRI (Figure 4.2) and has been taking measurements since 1993 (Table 4.4). The SAO station "Garrison" is 29 km north of KNRI and

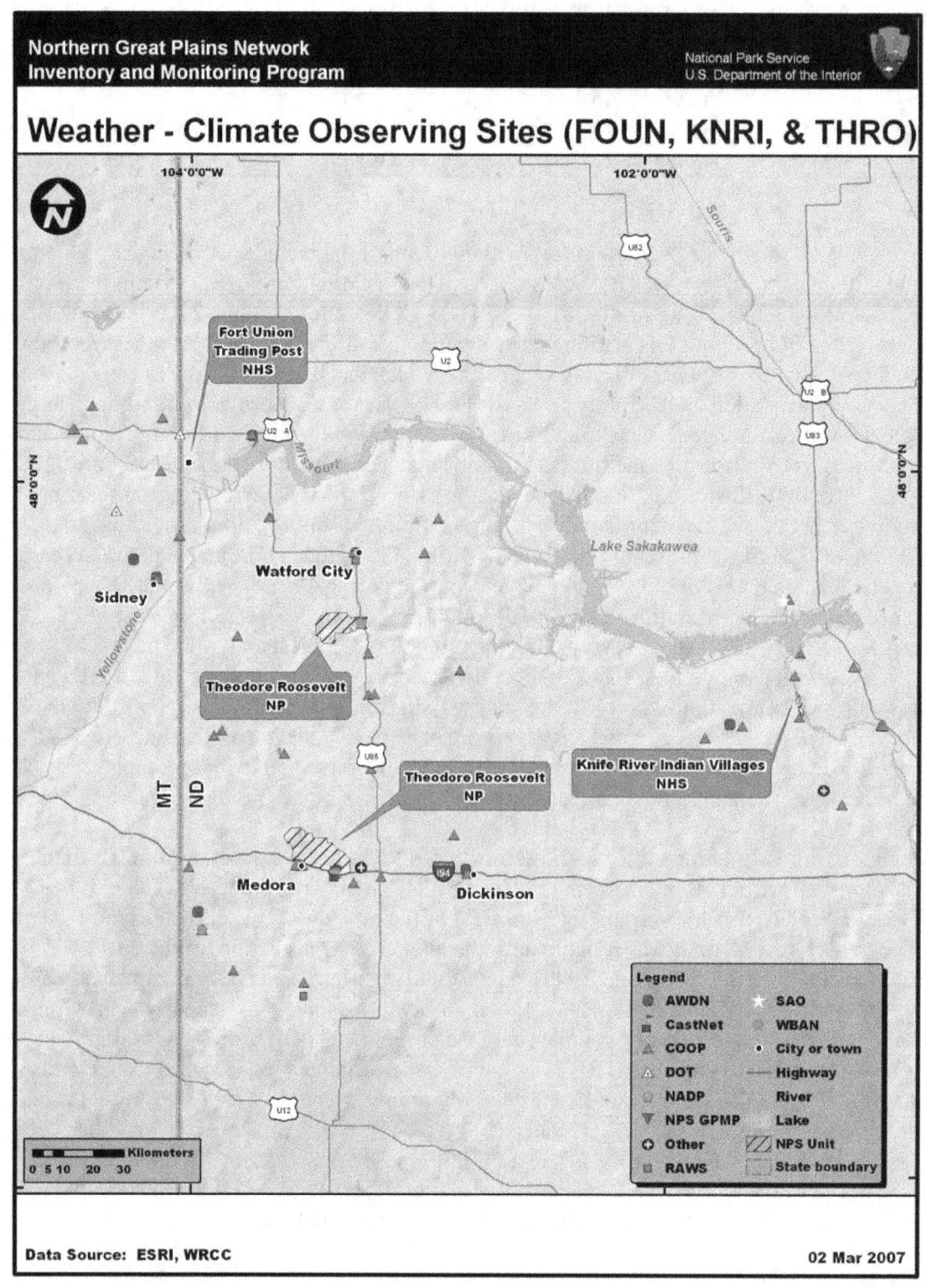

Figure 4.2. Station locations for the NGPN park units in North Dakota.

has been taking measurements since 1991. One CWOP station was identified at Center, 25 km south of KNRI.

Eight weather and climate stations were identified within the units of THRO (Table 4.4; Figure 4.2). Five of these stations are active currently. The north unit of THRO has four monitoring sites. The COOP station "Watford City 14 S" provides the primary climate record of all of THRO, as it has been active since 1951. The data record at this site is largely complete, with scattered data gaps. The last gap in the record occurred in October 2002. This COOP station is the only active climate monitoring site in the north unit of THRO. The remaining three stations we identified in the north unit were GPMP and NADP stations that are no longer active. The south unit of THRO also contains four weather/climate stations. The CASTNet station "Painted Canyon" has been taking measurements since 1998 and provides the primary source of automated weather data in all of THRO, along with the CRN station "Medora 7 E" (2004-present). The CASTNet site is collocated with a GPMP site which has also been operating since 1998. An NADP station (Theodore Roosevelt NP) has been operating in the south unit since 2001.

We identified three AWDN stations (two active) within 40 km of THRO units (Table 4.3). The AWDN station "Beach" is 36 km west of the south unit and started taking measurements in 1993. The AWDN station "Watford City" also became active in 1993; this station is 19 km north of the north unit. The AWDN station "Dickinson" is 38 km east of the south unit and started taking measurements in 1990.

Two other weather networks provide sources of near-real-time weather data for THRO. A GPS-MET station is located in Medora, about 4 km southwest of the south unit of THRO. Two active RAWS sites are located within 40 km of THRO units. Both of these sites have been active since 1997. "Sand Creek" is 40 km southwest of the south unit of THRO. The only data gap at "Sand Creek" occurred in November and December of 2002. "Watford City" is 17 km north of the north unit of THRO and had one significant data gap in September 1997.

4.2.3. Eastern Nebraska and South Dakota

Three stations (two active) were identified within MNRR (Table 4.5; Figure 4.3). All of these are COOP stations. "Niobrara," at Lewis and Clark Lake, provides the longest data record (1939-present) of the three stations. The data record at this site has scattered gaps; several gaps occurred in 2006 (April-June, August, October-December). The COOP station "Verdel 6 S," also at Lewis and Clark Lake, has been taking measurements since 1989.

Table 4.5. Weather and climate stations for NGPN park units in eastern Nebraska and South Dakota. Stations inside park units and within 40 km of the park unit boundary are included. Missing entries are indicated by "M".

Name	Lat.	Lon.	Elev. (m)	Network	Start	End	In Park?
Missouri National Recreational River (MNRR)							
Niobrara	42.747	-98.047	376	COOP	1/1/1939	Present	Yes
Verdel 6 S	42.733	-98.217	400	COOP	2/16/1989	Present	Yes
Yankton	42.867	-97.400	354	COOP	8/1/1921	1/31/1963	Yes
Beresford	43.067	-96.933	389	AWDN	1/1/1988	Present	No

Name	Lat.	Lon.	Elev. (m)	Network	Start	End	In Park?
Brunswick	42.350	-97.917	548	AWDN	6/29/1998	Present	No
Concord (NE)	42.383	-96.950	445	AWDN	7/16/1982	Present	No
Akron	42.837	-96.563	341	COOP	9/1/1900	Present	No
Alcester	43.029	-96.629	431	COOP	8/1/1948	11/22/2002	No
Alcester 4 ESE	42.983	-96.550	409	COOP	8/1/1956	6/30/1959	No
Alcester 4 SE	42.983	-96.567	427	COOP	9/1/1956	6/30/1959	No
Alcester 5 SE	42.967	-96.567	390	COOP	M	6/30/1959	No
Alcester 6 SE	42.967	-96.550	403	COOP	8/1/1956	10/31/1957	No
Alcester 7 ESE	42.967	-96.517	375	COOP	7/1/1956	6/30/1959	No
Alcester 7 SE	42.983	-96.517	378	COOP	7/1/1956	6/30/1959	No
Alcester 8 SE	42.967	-96.517	378	COOP	8/1/1956	10/31/1957	No
Alcester 9 SE	42.950	-96.517	363	COOP	8/1/1956	6/30/1959	No
Allen	42.417	-96.850	454	COOP	3/11/1992	12/1/1995	No
Armour	43.313	-98.349	460	COOP	4/1/1896	Present	No
Bazile Creek	42.750	-97.933	369	COOP	1/1/1978	9/30/1978	No
Bloomfield	42.594	-97.644	530	COOP	12/1/1905	Present	No
Bonesteel	43.078	-98.951	605	COOP	5/1/1956	7/1/2004	No
Bovee	43.317	-98.750	M	COOP	1/1/1950	11/30/1951	No
Butte	42.913	-98.851	552	COOP	5/1/1906	Present	No
Centerville 6 SE	43.043	-96.903	384	COOP	4/1/1897	Present	No
Coleridge	42.506	-97.209	488	COOP	11/1/1950	Present	No
Creighton	42.466	-97.903	497	COOP	1/1/1893	Present	No
Crofton	42.736	-97.497	427	COOP	8/1/1988	Present	No
Crofton 8 N	42.846	-97.473	383	COOP	11/19/2002	Present	No
Davis 2 SE	43.237	-96.983	374	COOP	8/1/1973	Present	No
Elk Point 13 NE	42.859	-96.582	366	COOP	4/1/1985	1/1/2001	No
Emerson	42.282	-96.726	440	COOP	1/1/1944	Present	No
Emerson 5 SE	42.233	-96.633	421	COOP	8/1/1948	7/1/1972	No
Fairfax	43.033	-98.883	589	COOP	9/2/1902	4/30/1956	No
Fairfax No. 2	43.031	-98.890	607	COOP	7/1/2004	Present	No
Gavins Point Dam	42.846	-97.473	383	COOP	1/1/1961	12/31/2002	No
Geddes	43.250	-98.683	491	COOP	8/13/1931	1/31/1950	No
Gross	42.944	-98.554	533	COOP	2/1/2001	Present	No
Hartington	42.617	-97.261	418	COOP	1/1/1893	Present	No
Haskell	42.381	-96.958	445	COOP	12/5/1997	Present	No
Hinton 4 W	42.650	-96.533	M	COOP	8/1/1948	8/23/1972	No
Homer 2	42.321	-96.488	335	COOP	1/15/1980	Present	No
Homer 3 NE	42.337	-96.432	330	COOP	3/1/1946	Present	No
James 1 NE	42.576	-96.304	353	COOP	4/1/1948	Present	No
Laurel	42.426	-97.091	454	COOP	8/1/1940	4/27/2000	No
Lynch	42.829	-98.458	424	COOP	4/1/1893	Present	No
Merrill	42.718	-96.249	363	COOP	5/1/1907	Present	No
Merrill 4 WSW	42.700	-96.333	421	COOP	5/1/1907	1/1/1978	No
NE Nebraska Exp. Stn.	42.380	-96.958	445	COOP	6/1/1957	12/5/1997	No
Newcastle	42.653	-96.873	411	COOP	8/25/1940	Present	No
Niobrara 2	42.717	-98.033	372	COOP	7/1/1972	4/2/1981	No

Name	Lat.	Lon.	Elev. (m)	Network	Start	End	In Park?
Niobrara 4 E	42.750	-97.933	369	COOP	1/11/1989	10/27/1997	No
Niobrara 6 WSW	42.729	-98.143	492	COOP	6/10/2005	Present	No
Oneill 19 NE	42.633	-98.358	570	COOP	7/7/2005	9/15/2006	No
Orchard	42.517	-98.268	524	COOP	4/17/2001	11/1/2004	No
Orchard 1 NW	42.349	-98.254	588	COOP	11/1/1971	10/1/2001	No
Pickstown	43.069	-98.533	454	COOP	1/1/1948	Present	No
Plainview	42.349	-97.793	512	COOP	4/1/1958	10/13/2000	No
Royal	42.333	-98.117	570	COOP	10/27/1950	10/19/1995	No
Royal 3 NE	42.379	-98.100	549	COOP	10/15/1987	Present	No
Santee	42.833	-97.850	375	COOP	M	Present	No
Scotland 5 NE	43.186	-97.635	356	COOP	7/1/1973	Present	No
Sioux City	42.396	-96.378	335	COOP	1/6/1997	Present	No
Sioux City	42.391	-96.379	334	COOP	1/1/1896	Present	No
Sioux City	42.500	-96.400	356	COOP	7/1/1889	12/31/1942	No
Sioux City 8 N	42.583	-96.433	354	COOP	2/1/1946	4/1/1983	No
Sioux City Hwy. 77 Br.	42.524	-96.480	303	COOP	2/2/1971	Present	No
Sioux City Perry Crk.	42.536	-96.411	366	COOP	2/1/1946	Present	No
South Sioux City	42.486	-96.414	322	COOP	2/1/1978	Present	No
Spencer 5 SSE	42.810	-98.656	466	COOP	1/1/1895	Present	No
St. James	42.733	-97.150	360	COOP	1/10/1989	5/1/1995	No
Tyndall	42.994	-97.862	433	COOP	1/1/1893	Present	No
Verdel 1 E	42.811	-98.176	385	COOP	1/1/1989	Present	No
Vermillion 2 SE	42.763	-96.919	363	COOP	1/1/1893	Present	No
Vermillion 2 W	42.783	-96.967	342	COOP	7/1/1972	9/5/1980	No
Vermillion 3 N	42.817	-96.924	342	COOP	9/28/1984	Present	No
Wagner	43.083	-98.297	436	COOP	2/1/1916	Present	No
Wakefield	42.267	-96.862	424	COOP	10/1/1894	Present	No
Wakonda 7 ESE	42.991	-96.964	351	COOP	12/1/1977	Present	No
Yankton 2 E	42.878	-97.363	360	COOP	1/1/1873	Present	No
CW3099 Sioux City	42.551	-96.453	431	CWOP	M	Present	No
WB0WNX Sioux City	42.557	-96.402	380	CWOP	M	Present	No
Lake Andes	43.259	-98.759	521	RAWS	11/1/2003	Present	No
Loess Hills TNC Broken	42.698	-96.582	335	RAWS	8/1/2004	Present	No
Sioux City	42.391	-96.379	334	SAO	1/1/1896	Present	No
Yankton 2 E	42.878	-97.363	360	SAO	1/1/1873	Present	No
Oneill	42.467	-98.533	603	WBAN	8/1/1953	9/30/1953	No
Sioux City	42.400	-96.383	339	WBAN	10/1/1942	3/31/1964	No

Niobrara National Scenic Riverway (NIOB)

Name	Lat.	Lon.	Elev. (m)	Network	Start	End	In Park?
Ainsworth	42.550	-99.817	765	AWDN	6/4/1984	Present	No
Higgins Ranch	42.833	-99.250	619	AWDN	7/13/2004	Present	No
Newport	42.583	-99.383	699	AWDN	8/12/2004	Present	No
Sparks	42.983	-100.200	772	AWDN	7/27/2004	Present	No
Ainsworth	42.552	-99.856	765	COOP	11/1/1905	Present	No
Atkinson	42.534	-98.978	643	COOP	6/1/1906	Present	No
Bassett	42.577	-99.540	707	COOP	1/1/1893	Present	No
Kilgore	42.950	-100.945	927	COOP	11/1/1997	Present	No

Name	Lat.	Lon.	Elev. (m)	Network	Start	End	In Park?
Mission 14 S	43.111	-100.608	856	COOP	8/1/1951	Present	No
Newport	42.601	-99.333	680	COOP	11/1/1895	Present	No
Norden 6 SSW	42.783	-100.033	643	COOP	7/1/1972	2/13/1998	No
Springview	42.822	-99.747	761	COOP	1/1/1893	Present	No
Valentine	42.571	-100.693	893	COOP	4/1/1937	Present	No
Valentine	42.875	-100.552	789	COOP	2/1/1998	Present	No
Valentine	42.878	-100.550	789	COOP	1/1/1886	Present	No
Wewela	43.017	-99.783	659	COOP	8/1/1951	6/14/1978	No
Ainsworth	42.583	-100.000	788	SAO	2/1/1943	2/28/1948	No
Ainsworth	42.583	-99.983	789	SAO	2/1/1955	Present	No
Valentine	42.878	-100.550	789	SAO	1/1/1886	Present	No

We identified three AWDN stations (all active) within 40 km of MNRR (Table 4.3). The AWDN station "Beresford" is 21 km northeast of MNRR and started taking measurements in 1988. The AWDN station "Brunswick" became active in 1998; this station is 30 km south of MNRR. The longest active AWDN station is "Concord (NE)," which is 30 km south of MNRR and started taking measurements in 1982.

We identified 73 COOP stations within 40 km of the boundaries of MNRR. Forty of these stations are active (Table 4.5). The longest record among these stations is at the COOP station "Yankton 2 E" (1873-present), which is 1 km north of MNRR. The data record at this station is very reliable. The COOP stations "Tyndall" (26 km north of MNRR) and "Hartington" (19 km south of MNRR) both became active in 1893 and both have reliable data records. The COOP station "Vermillion 2 SE," 3 km north of MNRR, also started taking measurements in 1893, but its data record does have scattered, small data gaps. The COOP station "Creighton" (1893-present) is 19 km south of MNRR and has provided a very reliable data record since 1948 for precipitation and since 1955 for temperature. The COOP station "Lynch" (1893-present), 11 km southwest of MNRR, has provided a very reliable precipitation measurements since 1948 and temperature measurements since 1965. The COOP station "Wakefield" is 38 km south of MNRR and provides a very reliable data record going back to 1894. The COOP station "Spencer 5 SSE" measures only precipitation and is 23 km southwest of MNRR. This site has been active since 1895, with a data record that is largely complete, with scattered data gaps. The COOP station "Sioux City" (1896-present) is 34 km southeast of MNRR and has provided a very reliable data record. "Armour" is a COOP station 32 km north of MNRR that started taking measurements in 1896. Its data record is largely complete, with scattered data gaps. "Centerville 6 SE" is a COOP station 19 km north of MNRR that started taking measurements in 1897. Its data record is largely complete, although a notable gap occurred in the record from December 1949 to September 1950. Several other COOP stations within 40 km of MNRR have long climate records, going back to the early twentieth century.

Two CWOP stations were identified within 40 km of MNRR (Table 4.5). Both of these are located near Sioux City (Figure 4.3).

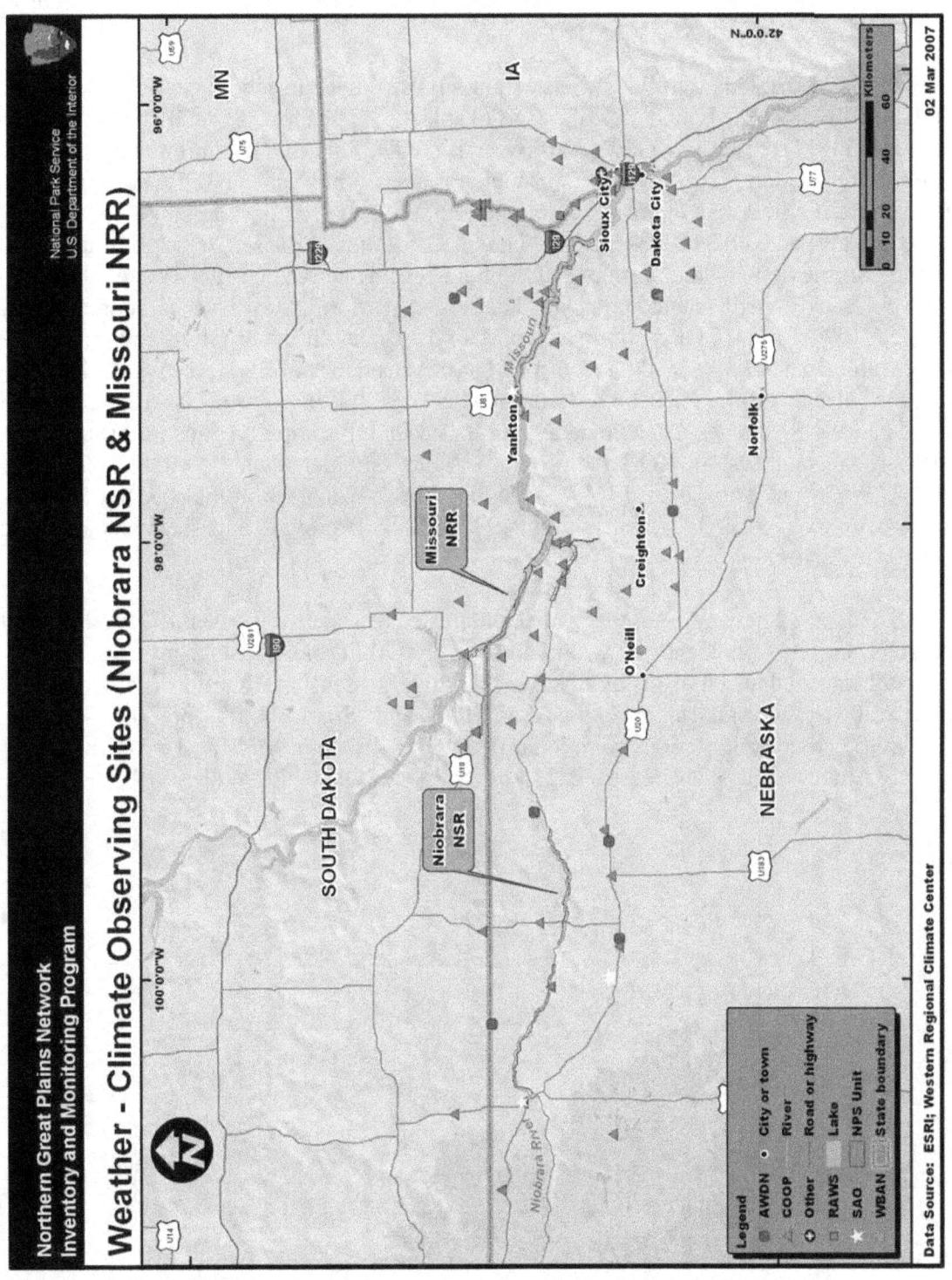

Figure 4.3. Station locations for the NGPN park units in eastern Nebraska and South Dakota.

47

Two RAWS stations were identified within 40 km of MNRR. "Lake Andes" is 27 km north of MNRR and provides a very reliable data record that goes back to 2003. "Loess Hills TNC Broken" is 9 km north of MNRR. Its data record had a gap in January and February of 2005. Besides these two RAWS stations, the other primary sources of near-real-time data for MNRR are two SAO stations, one in Sioux City and the other near Yankton (Yankton 2 E). Both of these SAO stations are collocated with previously-discussed COOP stations (Sioux City, Yankton 2 E).

No weather/climate stations were identified within NIOB. We identified 12 COOP stations (10 active) within 40 km of the boundaries of NIOB (Table 4.5). The closest COOP station to NIOB is "Valentine" (1998-present), which is 3 km west of NIOB. This COOP station may be identical to another COOP station named "Valentine," which is also 3 km west of NIOB (but slightly further away from NIOB than the first "Valentine" station) and provides the longest active climate record around NIOB (1886-present). The COOP stations "Bassett" (15 km south of NIOB) and "Springview" (9 km north of NIOB) both became active in 1893. The reliability of the data record at "Bassett" is uncertain. The data record at "Springview" has had numerous gaps since the late 1990s. The COOP station "Newport" is 19 km southeast of NIOB and started taking measurements in 1895. Its data record had numerous gaps during the 1950s but has been very reliable since that time. The COOP station "Ainsworth" (1905-present) is 21 km south of NIOB and has provided a very reliable data record. The COOP station "Atkinson" (1906-present) is 40 km southeast of NIOB and provides a fairly complete data record. Scattered gaps occurred at "Atkinson" prior to the 1940s. Since that time, the data record has become very reliable. A couple other COOP stations within 40 km of NIOB provide data records that go back to the 1950s or earlier.

The AWDN and SAO networks are the primary source of near-real-time weather data for NIOB. Four AWDN stations were identified within 40 km of NIOB (Table 4.5). "Ainsworth" (1984-present) is 21 km south of NIOB; "Higgins Ranch" (2004-present) is 9 km north of NIOB; "Newport" (2004-present) is 18 km southeast of NIOB; and "Sparks" (2004-present) is 12 km north of NIOB. Three SAO stations were identified within 40 km of MNRR. Two of these are still active. "Ainsworth" (1955-present) is 21 km south of NIOB while "Valentine" is 3 km west of NIOB.

5.0. Conclusions and Recommendations

We have based our findings on an examination of available climate records within NGPN units, discussions with NPS staff and other collaborators, and prior knowledge of the area. Here, we offer an evaluation and general comments pertaining to the status, prospects, and needs for climate-monitoring capabilities in NGPN. The NGPN has already acknowledged a need for additional coverage of weather and climate stations within its park units, in order to improve climate monitoring efforts across their network (Licht et al. 2005). Several opportunities have been identified for new station installations and are discussed below.

5.1. Northern Great Plains Inventory and Monitoring Network

We identified numerous long-term climate stations as well as real-time weather stations within 40 km of both MNRR and NIOB, providing ample sources of data for weather/climate monitoring efforts in these two park units. However, no real-time weather stations were identified within either park unit. Climate monitoring efforts could likely improve at both park units if this issue were to be resolved. At MNRR, a feasible strategy could be to install a real-time site such as an AWDN or RAWS station at one of the existing COOP sites we identified at Lewis and Clark Lake ("Niobrara" or "Verdel 6 S"). Both MNRR and NIOB have opportunities for setting up local climate transects along the Missouri River and Niobrara River. At NIOB, for instance, with an AWDN station (Higgins Ranch) already present near the east (downstream) end of the park unit, NIOB may want to consider a similar AWDN installation near the west end of the park unit. This would allow the park unit to conduct basic transect analyses such as monitoring diurnal wind and temperature cycles along the Niobrara River.

Both FOUS and KNRI have no real-time weather stations in or immediately near the park units. Both of these park units may want to consider installations of new automated stations to address this need. Since the AWDN and RAWS networks both have stations in North Dakota, they would be suitable candidates for new station installations. An AWDN installation may be more feasible at KNRI and would best be carried out by partnering with HPRCC, the primary agency that manages the AWDN network. Since no longer-term climate stations appear to be present in either FOUS or KNRI, these park units must rely heavily on outside sources of climate information. Therefore, climate monitoring activities at both park units will benefit by encouraging the continued operation of those climate stations that have been identified near the park units.

A very limited number of near-real-time weather stations have been identified for THRO. Most of the near-real-time stations we identified were in or near the south unit of THRO, with nothing being identified in the north unit or the Elkhorn Ranch site. Both the AWDN and RAWS networks already have a presence in the vicinity of THRO. Therefore, these networks would serve as suitable candidates for new station installations within THRO. The north unit of THRO contains significant topographical variations along the Little Missouri River Canyon. New station installations could be considered along the north unit's primary access road. This road passes through both riparian and canyon rim environments, each of which can have significantly different climate characteristics, so installations at both settings would need to be considered. Similarly, new weather station installations along the scenic loop through the south unit of

THRO could be valuable, as there are currently no near-real-time stations throughout much of the south unit, away from the visitor center.

Similar sampling gaps to THRO are found at BADL. Most of the weather/climate stations we identified in BADL are located near major road access points and the main visitor centers in the northeastern part of the park unit. Like THRO, BADL contains significant topographical variability, the associated microclimates of which are not currently sampled. Climate conditions in the southwestern portion of BADL remain largely unsampled at this point. The RAWS network already has a large presence in the area. Therefore, it could initially be beneficial for the NPS to work closely with local agencies to encourage the addition of new RAWS stations in southwestern BADL.

Many of the NGPN park units in and around the Black Hills (e.g., DETO, MORU, and WICA) have at least one longer climate record and one near-real-time station at the park unit. We encourage these park units to continue operating these valuable stations. Unlike most NGPN park units near the Black Hills, JECA has no weather/climate stations within its boundaries. Since there are no long-term climate records in the park unit, JECA must rely heavily on outside sources of reliable climate records for the area. Like FOUS and KNRI, climate monitoring activities at JECA will benefit by encouraging the continued operation of these long-term climate stations. The AWDN station "Jewel Cave," which is just outside JECA, is the primary source of automated weather data for the park unit. Therefore, its continued operation is likely of great importance to weather monitoring efforts in JECA.

Monitoring sites in AGFO include both long-term climate stations (e.g., the COOP station "Agate 3 E") and near-real-time weather stations (e.g., the CRN station "Harrison 20 SSE"). Despite the presence of significant data gaps at the COOP station "Agate 3 E," this station remains an important source for long-term climate data in AGFO and its continued operation should be encouraged. Local topography has a big influence on minimum temperatures in AGFO, with higher prairie settings, and warmer minimum temperatures, next to the Niobrara River valley and its cold-air drainages. Two near-real-time weather station installations could therefore be justified at AGFO, one sampling the higher rim environment and another sampling within the Niobrara River valley itself.

At SCBL, there are near-real-time stations but no long-term climate stations. Despite this lack of long-term climate records at SCBL, the park unit is located within a few kilometers of valuable climate records in the city of Scottsbluff. Local topography at SCBL and its associated microclimates could certainly justify the installation of one or two new near-real-time stations.

We only identified manual COOP stations inside FOLA. The closest reliable near-real-time weather data in the area comes from sites near Torrington, southeast of FOLA. Presently, one priority for climate monitoring efforts in FOLA would be to maintain the existing COOP (Old Fort Laramie) in order to build a reliable climate record for this park unit. The park unit may also want to consider installing an AWDN or RAWS station, if near-real-time weather data are desired for the park unit itself. Both networks are already present in this region.

5.2. Spatial Variations in Mean Climate

With local variations over short horizontal and vertical distances, topography introduces considerable fine-scale structure to mean climate (temperature and precipitation) within some NGPN park units, particularly those units in and around the Black Hills. Low-relief drainages within many of the NGPN park units can display significant nighttime temperature variations between the valleys and rims, variations that are often undersampled by current surface weather/climate station networks. Convective summer precipitation events also introduce a high level of spatial variability to precipitation characteristics in NGPN park units. Issues encountered in mapping mean climate are discussed in Appendix D and in Redmond et al. (2005).

For areas where new stations will be installed, if only a few new stations will be emplaced, the primary goal should be overall characterization of the main climate elements (temperature and precipitation and their joint relative, snow). This level of characterization generally requires that (a) stations should not be located in deep valley bottoms (cold air drainage pockets) or near excessively steep slopes and (b) stations should be distributed spatially in the major biomes of each park. If such stations already are present in the vicinity, then additional stations would be best used for two important and somewhat competing purposes: (a) add redundancy as backup for loss of data from current stations (or loss of the physical stations) or (b) provide added information on spatial heterogeneity in climate arising from topographic diversity.

5.3. Climate Change Detection

There is much interest in the adaptation of NGPN ecosystems in response to possible future climate change. In particular, there are concerns about habitat shifts and abilities of plant and animal communities to migrate in response to climate changes (Licht et al. 2005). The NGPN region is strongly affected by ENSO cycles. Future climate changes could affect the frequency, intensity, and duration of ENSO events in the area, which would in turn impact NGPN ecosystems.

The desire for credible, accurate, complete, and long-term climate records—from any location— cannot be overemphasized. Thus, this consideration always should have a high priority. However, because of spatial diversity in climate, monitoring that fills knowledge gaps and provides information on long-term temporal variability in short-distance relationships also will be valuable. We cannot be sure that climate variability and climate change will affect all parts of a given park unit equally. In fact, it is appropriate to speculate that this is not the case, and spatial variations in temporal variability extend to small spatial scales, a consequence of diversity within NGPN in both topography and in land use patterns.

5.4. Aesthetics

This issue arises frequently enough to deserve comment. Standards for quality climate measurements require open exposures away from heat sources, buildings, pavement, close vegetation and tall trees, and human intrusion (thus away from property lines). By their nature, sites that meet these standards are usually quite visible. In many settings (such as heavily forested areas) these sites also are quite rare, making them precisely the same places that managers wish to protect from aesthetic intrusion. The most suitable and scientifically defensible sites frequently are rejected as candidate locations for weather/climate stations. Most weather/climate stations, therefore, tend to be "hidden" but many of these hidden locations have inferior exposures. Some measure of compromise is nearly always called for in siting weather and climate stations.

The public has vast interest and curiosity in weather and climate, and within the NPS I&M networks, such measurements consistently rate near or at the top of desired public information. There seem to be many possible opportunities for exploiting and embracing this widespread interest within the interpretive mission of the NPS. One way to do this would be to highlight rather than hide these stations and educate the public about the need for adequate siting. A number of weather displays we have encountered during visits have proven inadvertently to serve as counterexamples for how measurements should not be made.

5.5. Information Access

Access to information promotes its use, which in turn promotes attention to station care and maintenance, better data, and more use. An end-to-end view that extends from sensing to decision support is far preferable to isolated and disconnected activities and aids the support infrastructure that is ultimately so necessary for successful, long-term climate monitoring.

Decisions about improvements in monitoring capacity are facilitated greatly by the ability to examine available climate information. Various methods are being created at WRCC to improve access to that information. Web pages providing historic and ongoing climate data, and information from NGPN park units, can be accessed at http://www.wrcc.dri.edu/nps. In the event that this URL changes, there still will be links from the main WRCC Web page entitled "Projects" under NPS.

The WRCC has been steadily developing software to summarize data from hourly sites. This has been occurring under the aegis of the RAWS program and a growing array of product generators ranging from daily and monthly data lists to wind diagrams and hourly frequency distributions. All park data are available to park personnel via an access code (needed only for data listings) that can be acquired by request. The WRCC RAWS Web page is located at http://www.wrcc.dri.edu/wraws or http://www.raws.dri.edu.

Web pages have been developed to provide access not only to historic and ongoing climate data and information from NGPN park units but also to climate-monitoring efforts for NGPN. These pages can be found through http://www.wrcc.dri.edu/nps.

Additional access to more standard climate information is accessible though the previously mentioned Web pages, as well as through http://www.wrcc.dri.edu/summary. These summaries are generally for COOP stations.

5.6. Summarized Conclusions and Recommendations

- NGPN has already recognized the importance of improved weather and climate station coverage within its park units (Licht et al. 2005).
- MNRR and NIOB have ample sources of both near-real-time stations and long-term climate stations near the park units, but not within the park units. MNRR could consider installing a near-real-time station (e.g., AWDN or RAWS) at existing COOP sites at Lewis

and Clark Lake. Climate transects may also be useful at both MNRR and NIOB. A new AWDN site near the west end of NIOB could be considered for such a purpose.

- FOUS and KNRI have no weather/climate stations, forcing these park units to rely heavily on outside sources of weather and climate data. New AWDN or RAWS station installations could be considered for both park units.
- No near-real-time weather stations have been identified for the north unit and the Elkhorn Ranch unit of THRO. New AWDN and RAWS station installations could be considered along the main roadways through all of the THRO units, sampling both riparian and canyon rim environments.
- Like THRO, local topography and its associated microclimates remain unsampled at both AGFO and SCBL. These park units could use installations of one or two new near-real-time weather stations.
- NGPN park units in and around Black Hills generally have at least one automated station and one long-term climate station. Neither type of station is present at JECA, causing the park unit to rely heavily on outside sources of weather and climate data.
- Weather and climate conditions in the southwestern portions of BADL are not currently sampled. The park unit could consider installing a RAWS station in this area.
- Climate monitoring efforts in NGPN will benefit by continuing the operation of those long-term climate stations identified in and near NGPN park units.

6.0 Literature Cited

American Association of State Climatologists. 1985. Heights and exposure standards for sensors on automated weather stations. The State Climatologist **9**.

Bachelet, D., J. M. Lenihan, C. Daly, and R. P. Neilson. 2000. Interactions between fire, grazing and climate change at Wind Cave National Park, SD. Ecological Modeling **134**:229-244.

Bevis, M., S. Businger, T. A. Herring, C. Rocken, R. A. Anthes, and R. H. Ware. 1992. GPS meteorology: remote sensing of the atmospheric water vapor using the global positioning system. Journal of Geophysical Research **97**:75–94.

Bonan, G. B. 2002. Ecological Climatology: Concepts and Applications. Cambridge University Press.

Borchert, J. R. 1950. The climate of the central North American grassland. Annals of the Association of American Geographers **40**:1-39.

Bunkers, M. J., J. R. Miller, Jr., and A. T. DeGaetano. 1996. An examination of El Niño-La Niña related precipitation and temperature anomalies across the Northern Plains. Journal of Climate **9**:147-160.

Bureau of Land Management. 1997. Remote Automatic Weather Station (RAWS) and Remote Environmental Monitoring Systems (REMS) standards. RAWS/REMS Support Facility, Boise, Idaho.

Chapin III, F. S., M. S. Torn, and M. Tateno. 1996. Principles of ecosystem sustainability. The American Naturalist **148**:1016-1037.

Clark, J. S., E. C. Grimm, J. J. Donovan, S. C. Fritz, D. R. Engstrom, and J. E. Almendinger. 2002. Drought cycles and landscape responses to past aridity on prairies of the Northern Great Plains. Ecology **83**:595-601.

Collins, S. L., and S. M. Glenn. 1995. Grassland ecosystem and landscape dynamics. Pages 128-156 *in* Joern, A., and K. H. Keeler, editors. The changing prairie: North American Grasslands. Oxford University Press, New York.

Daly, C., R. P. Neilson, and D. L. Phillips. 1994. A statistical-topographic model for mapping climatological precipitation over mountainous terrain. Journal of Applied Meteorology **33**:140-158.

Daly, C., W. P. Gibson, G. H. Taylor, G. L. Johnson, and P. Pasteris. 2002. A knowledge-based approach to the statistical mapping of climate. Climate Research **22**:99-113.

Doggett, M., C. Daly, J. Smith, W. Gibson, G. Taylor, G. Johnson, and P. Pasteris. 2004. High-resolution 1971-2000 mean monthly temperature maps for the western United States.

Fourteenth AMS Conf. on Applied Climatology, 84th AMS Annual Meeting. Seattle, Washington, American Meteorological Society, Boston, Massachusetts, January 2004, Paper 4.3, CD-ROM.

Duan, J., M. Bevis, P. Fang, Y. Bock, S. Chiswell, S. Businger, C. Rocken, F. Solheim, T. van Hove, R. Ware, and others. 1996. GPS meteorology: direct estimation of the absolute value of precipitable water. Journal of Applied Meteorology **35**:830-838.

Environmental Protection Agency. 1987. On-site meteorological program guidance for regulatory modeling applications. EPA-450/4-87-013. Environmental Protection Agency, Office of Air Quality Planning and Standards, Research Triangle Park, North Carolina.

Finklin, A. I., and W. C. Fischer. 1990. Weather station handbook –an interagency guide for wildland managers. NFES No. 2140. National Wildfire Coordinating Group, Boise, Idaho.

Gibson, W. P., C. Daly, T. Kittel, D. Nychka, C. Johns, N. Rosenbloom, A. McNab, and G. Taylor. 2002. Development of a 103-year high-resolution climate data set for the conterminous United States. Thirteenth AMS Conf. on Applied Climatology. Portland, Oregon, American Meteorological Society, Boston, MA, May 2002:181-183.

I&M. 2006. I&M Inventories home page. http://science.nature.nps.gov/im/inventory/index.cfm.

Jacobson, M. C., R. J. Charlson, H. Rodhe, and G. H. Orians. 2000. Earth System Science: From Biogeochemical Cycles to Global Change. Academic Press, San Diego.

Ji, L., and A. J. Peters. 2003. Assessing vegetation response to drought in the northern Great Plains using vegetation and drought indices. Remote Sensing of Environment **87**:85-98.

Karl, T. R., V. E. Derr, D. R. Easterling, C. K. Folland, D. J. Hoffman, S. Levitus, N. Nicholls, D. E. Parker, and G. W. Withee. 1996. Critical issues for long-term climate monitoring. Pages 55-92 *in* T. R. Karl, editor. Long Term Climate Monitoring by the Global Climate Observing System, Kluwer Publishing.

Licht, D. S., and others. 2005. Northern Great Plains I&M Network: Vital Signs Monitoring Plan. Northern Great Plains Network, National Park Service.

Mock, C. J. 1991. Drought and precipitation fluctuations in the Great Plains during the late nineteenth century. Great Plains Research **1**:26-57.

National Assessment Synthesis Team. 2001. Climate Change Impacts on the United States: The Potential Consequences of Climate Variability and Change, Report for the U.S. Global Change Research Program. Cambridge University Press, Cambridge, UK.

National Research Council. 2001. A Climate Services Vision: First Steps Toward the Future. National Academies Press, Washington, D.C.

National Wildfire Coordinating Group. 2004. National fire danger rating system weather station standards. Report PMS 426.3. National Wildfire Coordinating Group, Boise, Idaho.

Neilson, R. P. 1987. Biotic regionalization and climatic controls in western North America. Vegetatio **70**:135-147.

Oakley, K. L., L. P. Thomas, and S. G. Fancy. 2003. Guidelines for long-term monitoring protocols. Wildlife Society Bulletin **31**:1000-1003.

Ojima, D., L. Garcia, E. Eigaali, K. Miller, T. G. F. Kittel, and J. Lackelt. 1999. Potential climate change impacts on water resources in the Great Plains. Journal of the American Water Resources Association **35**:1443-1454.

Redmond, K. T., D. B. Simeral, and G. D. McCurdy. 2005. Climate monitoring for southwest Alaska national parks: network design and site selection. Report 05-01. Western Regional Climate Center, Reno, Nevada.

Rodriguez-Iturbe, I. 2000. Ecohydrology: A hydrologic perspective of climate-soil-vegetation dynamics. Water Resources Research **36**:3-9.

Schlesinger, W. H. 1997. Biogeochemistry: An Analysis of Global Change. Academic Press, San Diego.

Schubert, S. D., M. J. Suarez, P. J. Pegion, R. D. Koster, and J. T. Bacmeister. 2004. Causes of long-term drought in the U.S. Great Plains. Journal of Climate **17**:485-503.

Shapley, M. D., W. C. Johnson, D. R. Engstrom, and W. R. Osterkamp. 2005. Late-Holocene flooding and drought in the Northern Great Plains, USA, reconstructed from tree rings, lake sediments and ancient shorelines. Holocene **15**:29-41.

Tanner, B. D. 1990. Automated weather stations. Remote Sensing Reviews **5**:73-98.

Weaver, J. E. 1943. Resurvey of grasses, forbs,, and underground plant parts at the end of the great drought. Ecological Monographs **13**:63-117.

Whiteman, C. D. 1973. Variability of High Plains precipitation. Technical Report NOAA TR ERL 287-APCL 31. United States National Oceanic and Atmospheric Administration. Environmental Research Labs., Boulder, Colorado.

Wilken, G. C. 1988. Climate and weather of the Great Plains. Pages 18-20 *in* Impacts of the Conservation Reserve Program in the Great Plains: symposium proceedings, September 16-18, 1987, Denver, Colorado.

World Meteorological Organization. 1983. Guide to meteorological instruments and methods of observation, No. 8, 5th edition, World Meteorological Organization, Geneva, Switzerland.

World Meteorological Organization. 2005. Organization and planning of intercomparisons of rainfall intensity gauges. World Meteorological Organization, Geneva, Switzerland.

Yuan, L. L., R. A. Anthes, R. H. Ware, C. Rocken, W. D. Bonner, M. G. Bevis, and S. Businger. 1993. Sensing climate change using the global positioning system. Journal of Geophysical Research **98**:14925-14937.

Appendix A. Glossary

Climate—Complete and entire ensemble of statistical descriptors of temporal and spatial properties comprising the behavior of the atmosphere. These descriptors include means, variances, frequency distributions, autocorrelations, spatial correlations and other patterns of association, temporal lags, and element-to-element relationships. The descriptors have a physical basis in flows and reservoirs of energy and mass. Climate and weather phenomena shade gradually into each other and are ultimately inseparable.

Climate Element—(same as Weather Element) Attribute or property of the state of the atmosphere that is measured, estimated, or derived. Examples of climate elements include temperature, wind speed, wind direction, precipitation amount, precipitation type, relative humidity, dewpoint, solar radiation, snow depth, soil temperature at a given depth, etc. A derived element is a function of other elements (like degree days or number of days with rain) and is not measured directly with a sensor. The terms "parameter" or "variable" are not used to describe elements.

Climate Network—Group of climate stations having a common purpose; the group is often owned and maintained by a single organization.

Climate Station—Station where data are collected to track atmospheric conditions over the long-term. Often, this station operates to additional standards to verify long-term consistency. For these stations, the detailed circumstances surrounding a set of measurements (siting and exposure, instrument changes, etc.) are important.

Data—Measurements specifying the state of the physical environment. Does not include metadata.

Data Inventory—Information about overall data properties for each station within a weather or climate network. A data inventory may include start/stop dates, percentages of available data, breakdowns by climate element, counts of actual data values, counts or fractions of data types, etc. These properties must be determined by actually reading the data and thus require the data to be available, accessible, and in a readable format.

NPS I&M Network—A set of NPS park units grouped by a common theme, typically by natural resource and/or geographic region.

Metadata—Information necessary to interpret environmental data properly, organized as a history or series of snapshots—data about data. Examples include details of measurement processes, station circumstances and exposures, assumptions about the site, network purpose and background, types of observations and sensors, pre-treatment of data, access information, maintenance history and protocols, observational methods, archive locations, owner, and station start/end period.

Quality Assurance—Planned and systematic set of activities to provide adequate confidence that products and services are resulting in credible and correct information. Includes quality control.

Quality Control—Evaluation, assessment, and improvement of imperfect data by utilizing other imperfect data.

Station Inventory—Information about a set of stations obtained from metadata that accompany the network or networks. A station inventory can be compiled from direct and indirect reports prepared by others.

Weather—Instantaneous state of the atmosphere at any given time, mainly with respect to its effects on biological activities. As distinguished from climate, weather consists of the short-term (minutes to days) variations in the atmosphere. Popularly, weather is thought of in terms of temperature, precipitation, humidity, wind, sky condition, visibility, and cloud conditions.

Weather Element (same as Climate Element)—Attribute or property of the state of the atmosphere that is measured, estimated, or derived. Examples of weather elements include temperature, wind speed, wind direction, precipitation amount, precipitation type, relative humidity, dewpoint, solar radiation, snow depth, soil temperature at a given depth, etc. A derived weather element is a function of other elements (like degree days or number of days with rain) and is not measured directly. The terms "parameter" and "variable" are not used to describe weather elements.

Weather Network—Group of weather stations usually owned and maintained by a particular organization and usually for a specific purpose.

Weather Station—Station where collected data are intended for near-real-time use with less need for reference to long-term conditions. In many cases, the detailed circumstances of a set of measurements (siting and exposure, instrument changes, etc.) from weather stations are not as important as for climate stations.

Appendix B. Climate-monitoring principles

Since the late 1990s, frequent references have been made to a set of climate-monitoring principles enunciated in 1996 by Tom Karl, director of the NOAA NCDC in Asheville, North Carolina. These monitoring principles also have been referred to informally as the "Ten Commandments of Climate Monitoring." Both versions are given here. In addition, these principles have been adopted by the Global Climate Observing System (GCOS 2004).

(Compiled by Kelly Redmond, Western Regional Climate Center, Desert Research Institute, August 2000.)

B.1. Full Version (Karl et al. 1996)

B.1.1. Effects on climate records of instrument changes, observing practices, observation locations, sampling rates, etc., must be known before such changes are implemented. This can be ascertained through a period where overlapping measurements from old and new observing systems are collected or sometimes by comparing the old and new observing systems with a reference standard. Site stability for in situ measurements, both in terms of physical location and changes in the nearby environment, also should be a key criterion in site selection. Thus, many synoptic network stations, which are primarily used in weather forecasting but also provide valuable climate data, and dedicated climate stations intended to be operational for extended periods must be subject to this policy.

B.1.2. Processing algorithms and changes in these algorithms must be well documented. Documentation should be carried with the data throughout the data-archiving process.

B.1.3. Knowledge of instrument, station, and/or platform history is essential for interpreting and using the data. Changes in instrument sampling time, local environmental conditions for in situ measurements, and other factors pertinent to interpreting the observations and measurements should be recorded as a mandatory part in the observing routine and be archived with the original data.

B.1.4. In situ and other observations with a long, uninterrupted record should be maintained. Every effort should be applied to protect the data sets that have provided long-term, homogeneous observations. "Long-term" for space-based measurements is measured in decades, but for more conventional measurements, "long-term" may be a century or more. Each element in the observational system should develop a list of prioritized sites or observations based on their contribution to long-term climate monitoring.

B.1.5. Calibration, validation, and maintenance facilities are critical requirements for long-term climatic data sets. Homogeneity in the climate record must be assessed routinely, and corrective action must become part of the archived record.

B.1.6. Where feasible, some level of "low-technology" backup to "high-technology" observing systems should be developed to safeguard against unexpected operational failures.

B.1.7. Regions having insufficient data, variables and regions sensitive to change, and key measurements lacking adequate spatial and temporal resolution should be given the highest priority in designing and implementing new climate-observing systems.

B.1.8. Network designers and instrument engineers must receive long-term climate requirements at the outset of the network design process. This is particularly important because most observing systems have been designed for purposes other than long-term climate monitoring. Instruments must possess adequate accuracy with biases small enough to document climate variations and changes.

B.1.9. Much of the development of new observational capabilities and the evidence supporting the value of these observations stem from research-oriented needs or programs. A lack of stable, long-term commitment to these observations and lack of a clear transition plan from research to operations are two frequent limitations in the development of adequate, long-term monitoring capabilities. Difficulties in securing a long-term commitment must be overcome in order to improve the climate-observing system in a timely manner with minimal interruptions.

B.1.10. Data management systems that facilitate access, use, and interpretation are essential. Freedom of access, low cost, mechanisms that facilitate use (directories, catalogs, browse capabilities, availability of metadata on station histories, algorithm accessibility and documentation, etc.) and quality control should guide data management. International cooperation is critical for successful management of data used to monitor long-term climate change and variability.

B.2. Abbreviated version, "Ten Commandments of Climate Monitoring"

B.2.1. Assess the impact of new climate-observing systems or changes to existing systems before they are implemented.

"Thou shalt properly manage network change." (assess effects of proposed changes)

B.2.2. Require a suitable period where measurement from new and old climate-observing systems will overlap.

"Thou shalt conduct parallel testing." (compare old and replacement systems)

B.2.3. Treat calibration, validation, algorithm-change, and data-homogeneity assessments with the same care as the data.

"Thou shalt collect metadata." (fully document system and operating procedures)

B.2.4. Verify capability for routinely assessing the quality and homogeneity of the data including high-resolution data for extreme events.

"Thou shalt assure data quality and continuity." (assess as part of routine operating procedures)

B.2.5. Integrate assessments like those conducted by the International Panel on Climate Change into global climate-observing priorities.

"Thou shalt anticipate the use of data." (integrated environmental assessment; component in operational plan for system)

B.2.6. Maintain long-term weather and climate stations.

"Thou shalt worship historic significance." (maintain homogeneous data sets from long–term, climate-observing systems)

B.2.7. Place high priority on increasing observations in regions lacking sufficient data and in regions sensitive to change and variability.

"Thou shalt acquire complementary data." (new sites to fill observational gaps)

B.2.8. Provide network operators, designers, and instrument engineers with long-term requirements at the outset of the design and implementation phases for new systems.

"Thou shalt specify requirements for climate observation systems." (application and usage of observational data)

B.2.9. Carefully consider the transition from research-observing system to long-term operation.

"Thou shalt have continuity of purpose." (stable long-term commitments)

B.2.10. Focus on data-management systems that facilitate access, use, and interpretation of weather data and metadata.

"Thou shalt provide access to data and metadata." (readily available weather and climate information)

B.3. Literature Cited

Karl, T. R., V. E. Derr, D. R. Easterling, C. K. Folland, D. J. Hoffman, S. Levitus, N. Nicholls, D. E. Parker, and G. W. Withee. 1996. Critical Issues for Long-Term Climate Monitoring. Pages 55-92 *in* T. R. Karl, editor. Long Term Climate Monitoring by the Global Climate Observing System, Kluwer Publishing.

Global Climate Observing System. 2004. Implementation Plan for the Global Observing System for Climate in Support of the UNFCCC. GCOS-92, WMO/TD No. 1219, World Meteorological Organization, Geneva, Switzerland.

Appendix C. Factors in operating a weather/ climate network

C.1. Climate versus Weather

- Climate measurements require _consistency through time._

C.2. Network Purpose

- Anticipated or desired lifetime.
- Breadth of network mission (commitment by needed constituency).
- Dedicated constituency—no network survives without a dedicated constituency.

C.3. Site Identification and Selection

- Spanning gradients in climate or biomes with transects.
- Issues regarding representative spatial scale—site uniformity versus site clustering.
- Alignment with and contribution to network mission.
- Exposure—ability to measure representative quantities.
- Logistics—ability to service station (Always or only in favorable weather?).
- Site redundancy (positive for quality control, negative for extra resources).
- Power—is AC needed?
- Site security—is protection from vandalism needed?
- Permitting often a major impediment and usually underestimated.

C.4. Station Hardware

- Survival—weather is the main cause of lost weather/climate data.
- Robustness of sensors—ability to measure and record in any condition.
- Quality—distrusted records are worthless and a waste of time and money.
  - High quality—will cost up front but pays off later.
  - Low quality—may provide a lower start-up cost but will cost more later (low cost can be expensive).
- Redundancy—backup if sensors malfunction.
- Ice and snow—measurements are much more difficult than rain measurements.
- Severe environments (expense is about two–three times greater than for stations in more benign settings).

C.5. Communications

- Reliability—live data have a much larger constituency.
- One-way or two-way.
  - Retrieval of missed transmissions.
  - Ability to reprogram data logger remotely.
  - Remote troubleshooting abilities.
  - Continuing versus one-time costs.
- Back-up procedures to prevent data loss during communication outages.
- Live communications increase problems but also increase value.

C.6. Maintenance

- Main reason why networks fail (and most networks do eventually fail!).
- Key issue with nearly every network.
- Who will perform maintenance?
- Degree of commitment and motivation to contribute.
- Periodic? On-demand as needed? Preventive?
- Equipment change-out schedules and upgrades for sensors and software.
- Automated stations require skilled and experienced labor.
- Calibration—sensors often drift (climate).
- Site maintenance essential (constant vegetation, surface conditions, nearby influences).
- Typical automated station will cost about $2K per year to maintain.
- Documentation—photos, notes, visits, changes, essential for posterity.
- Planning for equipment life cycle and technological advances.

C.7. Maintaining Programmatic Continuity and Corporate Knowledge

- Long-term vision and commitment needed.
- Institutionalizing versus personalizing—developing appropriate dependencies.

C.8. Data Flow

- Centralized ingest?
- Centralized access to data and data products?
- Local version available?
- Contract out work or do it yourself?
- Quality control of data.
- Archival.
- Metadata—historic information, not a snapshot. Every station should collect metadata.
- Post-collection processing, multiple data-ingestion paths.

C.9. Products

- Most basic product consists of the data values.
- Summaries.
- Write own applications or leverage existing mechanisms?

C.10. Funding

- Prototype approaches as proof of concept.
- Linking and leveraging essential.
- Constituencies—every network needs a constituency.
- Bridging to practical and operational communities? Live data needed.
- Bridging to counterpart research efforts and initiatives—funding source.
- Creativity, resourcefulness, and persistence usually are essential to success.

C.11. Final Comments

- Deployment is by far the easiest part in operating a network.
- Maintenance is the main issue.
- Best analogy: Operating a network is like raising a child; it requires constant attention.

Source: Western Regional Climate Center (WRCC)

Appendix D. General design considerations for weather/climate-monitoring programs

The process for designing a climate-monitoring program benefits from anticipating design and protocol issues discussed here. Much of this material is been excerpted from a report addressing the Channel Islands National Park (Redmond and McCurdy 2005), where an example is found illustrating how these factors can be applied to a specific setting. Many national park units possess some climate or meteorology feature that sets them apart from more familiar or "standard" settings.

D.1. Introduction

There are several criteria that must be used in deciding to deploy new stations and where these new stations should be sited.

- Where are existing stations located?
- Where have data been gathered in the past (discontinued locations)?
- Where would a new station fill a knowledge gap about basic, long-term climatic averages for an area of interest?
- Where would a new station fill a knowledge gap about how climate behaves over time?
- As a special case for behavior over time, what locations might be expected to show a more sensitive response to climate change?
- How do answers to the preceding questions depend on the climate element? Are answers the same for precipitation, temperature, wind, snowfall, humidity, etc.?
- What role should manual measurements play? How should manual measurements interface with automated measurements?
- Are there special technical or management issues, either present or anticipated in the next 5–15 years, requiring added climate information?
- What unique information is provided in addition to information from existing sites? "Redundancy is bad."
- What nearby information is available to estimate missing observations because observing systems always experience gaps and lose data? "Redundancy is good."
- How would logistics and maintenance affect these decisions?

In relation to the preceding questions, there are several topics that should be considered. The following topics are not listed in a particular order.

D.1.1. Network Purpose

Humans seem to have an almost reflexive need to measure temperature and precipitation, along with other climate elements. These reasons span a broad range from utilitarian to curiosity-driven. Although there are well-known recurrent patterns of need and data use, new uses are always appearing. The number of uses ranges in the thousands. Attempts have been made to categorize such uses (see NRC 1998; 2001). Because climate measurements are accumulated over a long time, they should be treated as multi-purpose and should be undertaken in a manner that serves the widest possible applications. Some applications remain constant, while others rise and fall in importance. An insistent issue today may subside, while the next pressing issue of tomorrow barely may be anticipated. The notion that humans might affect the climate of the entire Earth was nearly unimaginable when the national USDA (later NOAA) cooperative weather network began in the late 1800s. Abundant experience has shown, however, that there always will be a demand for a history record of climate measurements and their properties. Experience also shows that there is an expectation that climate measurements will be taken and made available to the general public.

An exhaustive list of uses for data would fill many pages and still be incomplete. In broad terms, however, there are needs to document environmental conditions that disrupt or otherwise affect park operations (e.g., storms and droughts). Design and construction standards are determined by climatological event frequencies that exceed certain thresholds. Climate is a determinant that sometimes attracts and sometimes discourages visitors. Climate may play a large part in the park experience (e.g., Death Valley and heat are nearly synonymous). Some park units are large enough to encompass spatial or elevation diversity in climate and the sequence of events can vary considerably inside or close to park boundaries. That is, temporal trends and statistics may not be the same everywhere, and this spatial structure should be sampled. The granularity of this structure depends on the presence of topography or large climate gradients or both, such as that found along the U.S. West Coast in summer with the rapid transition from the marine layer to the hot interior.

Plant and animal communities and entire ecosystems react to every nuance in the physical environment. No aspect of weather and climate goes undetected in the natural world. Wilson (1998) proposed "an informal rule of biological evolution" that applies here: "If an organic sensor can be imagined that is capable of detecting any particular environmental signal, a species exists somewhere that possesses this sensor." Every weather and climate event, whether dull or extraordinary to humans, matters to some organism. Dramatic events and creeping incremental change both have consequences to living systems. Extreme events or disturbances can "reset the clock" or "shake up the system" and lead to reverberations that last for years to centuries or longer. Slow change can carry complex nonlinear systems (e.g., any living assemblage) into states where chaotic transitions and new behavior occur. These changes are seldom predictable, typically are observed after the fact, and understood only in retrospect. Climate changes may not be exciting, but as a well-known atmospheric scientist, Mike Wallace, from the University of Washington once noted, "subtle does not mean unimportant."

Thus, individuals who observe the climate should be able to record observations accurately and depict both rapid and slow changes. In particular, an array of artificial influences easily can confound detection of slow changes. The record as provided can contain both real climate variability (that took place in the atmosphere) and fake climate variability (that arose directly from the way atmospheric changes were observed and recorded). As an example, trees growing near a climate station with an excellent anemometer will make it appear that the wind gradually slowed down over many years. Great care must be taken to protect against sources of fake climate variability on the longer-time scales of years to decades. Processes leading to the observed climate are not stationary; rather these processes draw from probability distributions that vary with time. For this reason, climatic time series do not exhibit statistical stationarity. The implications are manifold. There are no true climatic "normals" to which climate inevitably must return. Rather, there are broad ranges of climatic conditions. Climate does not demonstrate exact repetition but instead continual fluctuation and sometimes approximate repetition. In addition, there is always new behavior waiting to occur. Consequently, the business of climate monitoring is never finished, and there is no point where we can state confidently that "enough" is known.

D.1.2. Robustness
The most frequent cause for loss of weather data is the weather itself, the very thing we wish to record. The design of climate and weather observing programs should consider the meteorological equivalent of "peaking power" employed by utilities. Because environmental disturbances have significant effects on ecologic systems, sensors, data loggers, and communications networks should be able to function during the most severe conditions that realistically can be anticipated over the next 50–100 years. Systems designed in this manner are less likely to fail under more ordinary conditions, as well as more likely to transmit continuous, quality data for both tranquil and active periods.

D.1.3. Weather versus Climate
For "weather" measurements, pertaining to what is approximately happening here and now, small moves and changes in exposure are not as critical. For "climate" measurements, where values from different points in time are compared, siting and exposure are critical factors, and it is vitally important that the observing circumstances remain essentially unchanged over the duration of the station record.

Station moves can affect different elements to differing degrees. Even small moves of several meters, especially vertically, can affect temperature records. Hills and knolls act differently from the bottoms of small swales, pockets, or drainage channels (Whiteman 2000; Geiger et al. 2003). Precipitation is probably less subject to change with moves of 50–100 m than other elements (that is, precipitation has less intrinsic variation in small spaces) except if wind flow over the gauge is affected.

D.1.4. Physical Setting
Siting and exposure, and their continuity and consistency through time, significantly influence the climate records produced by a station. These two terms have overlapping connotations. We use the term "siting" in a more general sense, reserving the term "exposure" generally for the particular circumstances affecting the ability of an instrument to record measurements that are representative of the desired spatial or temporal scale.

D.1.5. Measurement Intervals
Climatic processes occur continuously in time, but our measurement systems usually record in discrete chunks of time: for example, seconds, hours, or days. These measurements often are referred to as "systematic" measurements. Interval averages may hide active or interesting periods of highly intense activity. Alternatively, some systems record "events" when a certain threshold of activity is exceeded (examples: another millimeter of precipitation has fallen, another kilometer of wind has moved past, the temperature has changed by a degree, a gust higher than 9.9 m/s has been measured). When this occurs, measurements from all sensors are reported. These measurements are known as "breakpoint" data. In relatively unchanging conditions (long calm periods or rainless weeks, for example), event recorders should send a signal that they are still "alive and well." If systematic recorders are programmed to note and periodically report the highest, lowest, and mean value within each time interval, the likelihood

is reduced that interesting behavior will be glossed over or lost. With the capacity of modern data loggers, it is recommended to record and report extremes within the basic time increment (e.g., hourly or 10 minutes). This approach also assists quality-control procedures.

There is usually a trade-off between data volume and time increment, and most automated systems now are set to record approximately hourly. A number of field stations maintained by WRCC are programmed to record in 5- or 10-minute increments, which readily serve to construct an hourly value. However, this approach produces 6–12 times as much data as hourly data. These systems typically do not record details of events at sub-interval time scales, but they easily can record peak values, or counts of threshold exceedance, within the time intervals.

Thus, for each time interval at an automated station, we recommend that several kinds of information—mean or sum, extreme maximum and minimum, and sometimes standard deviation—be recorded. These measurements are useful for quality control and other purposes. Modern data loggers and office computers have quite high capacity. Diagnostic information indicating the state of solar chargers or battery voltages and their extremes is of great value. This topic will be discussed in greater detail in a succeeding section.

Automation also has made possible adaptive or intelligent monitoring techniques where systems vary the recording rate based on detection of the behavior of interest by the software. Sub-interval behavior of interest can be masked on occasion (e.g., a 5-minute extreme downpour with high-erosive capability hidden by an innocuous hourly total). Most users prefer measurements that are systematic in time because they are much easier to summarize and manipulate.

For breakpoint data produced by event reporters, there also is a need to send periodically a signal that the station is still functioning, even though there is nothing more to report. "No report" does not necessarily mean "no data," and it is important to distinguish between the actual observation that was recorded and the content of that observation (e.g., an observation of "0.00" is not the same as "no observation").

D.1.6. Mixed Time Scales
There are times when we may wish to combine information from radically different scales. For example, over the past 100 years we may want to know how the frequency of 5-minute precipitation peaks has varied or how the frequency of peak 1-second wind gusts have varied. We may also want to know over this time if nearby vegetation gradually has grown up to increasingly block the wind or to slowly improve precipitation catch. Answers to these questions require knowledge over a wide range of time scales.

D.1.7. Elements
For manual measurements, the typical elements recorded included temperature extremes, precipitation, and snowfall/snow depth. Automated measurements typically include temperature, precipitation, humidity, wind speed and direction, and solar radiation. An exception to this exists in very windy locations where precipitation is difficult to measure accurately. Automated measurements of snow are improving, but manual measurements are still preferable, as long as shielding is present. Automated measurement of frozen precipitation presents numerous challenges that have not been resolved fully, and the best gauges are quite expensive ($3–8K).

Soil temperatures also are included sometimes. Soil moisture is extremely useful, but measurements are not made at many sites. In addition, care must be taken in the installation and maintenance of instruments used in measuring soil moisture. Soil properties vary tremendously in short distances as well, and it is often very difficult ("impossible") to accurately document these variations (without digging up all the soil!). In cooler climates, ultrasonic sensors that detect snow depth are becoming commonplace.

D.1.8. Wind Standards

Wind varies the most in the shortest distance, since it always decreases to zero near the ground and increases rapidly (approximately logarithmically) with height near the ground. Changes in anemometer height obviously will affect distribution of wind speed as will changes in vegetation, obstructions such as buildings, etc. A site that has a 3-m (10-ft) mast clearly will be less windy than a site that has a 6-m (20-ft) or 10-m (33-ft) mast. Historically, many U.S. airports (FAA and NWS) and most current RAWS sites have used a standard 6-m (20-ft) mast for wind measurements. Some NPS RAWS sites utilize shorter masts. Over the last decade, as Automated Surface Observing Systems (ASOSs, mostly NWS) and Automated Weather Observing Systems (AWOSs, mostly FAA) have been deployed at most airports, wind masts have been raised to 8 or 10 m (26 or 33 ft), depending on airplane clearance. The World Meteorological Organization recommends 10 m as the height for wind measurements (WMO 1983; 2005), and more groups are migrating slowly to this standard. The American Association of State Climatologists (AASC 1985) have recommended that wind be measured at 3 m, a standard geared more for agricultural applications than for general purpose uses where higher levels usually are preferred. Different anemometers have different starting thresholds; therefore, areas that frequently experience very light winds may not produce wind measurements thus affecting long-term mean estimates of wind speed. For both sustained winds (averages over a short interval of 2–60 minutes) and especially for gusts, the duration of the sampling interval makes a considerable difference. For the same wind history, 1–second gusts are higher than gusts averaging 3 seconds, which in turn are greater than 5-second averages, so that the same sequence would be described with different numbers (all three systems and more are in use). Changes in the averaging procedure, or in height or exposure, can lead to "false" or "fake" climate change with no change in actual climate. Changes in any of these should be noted in the metadata.

D.1.9. Wind Nomenclature

Wind is a vector quantity having a direction and a speed. Directions can be two- or three-dimensional; they will be three-dimensional if the vertical component is important. In all common uses, winds always are denoted by the direction they blow *from* (north wind or southerly breeze). This convention exists because wind often brings weather, and thus our attention is focused upstream. However, this approach contrasts with the way ocean currents are viewed. Ocean currents usually are denoted by the direction they are moving *towards* (eastward current moves from west to east). In specialized applications (such as in atmospheric modeling), wind velocity vectors point in the direction that the wind is blowing. Thus, a southwesterly wind (from the southwest) has both northward and eastward (to the north and to the east) components. Except near mountains, wind cannot blow up or down near the ground, so the vertical component of wind often is approximated as zero, and the horizontal component is emphasized.

D.1.10. Frozen Precipitation

Frozen precipitation is more difficult to measure than liquid precipitation, especially with automated techniques. Sevruk and Harmon (1984), Goodison et al. (1998), and Yang et al. (1998; 2001) provide many of the reasons to explain this. The importance of frozen precipitation varies greatly from one setting to another. This subject was discussed in greater detail in a related inventory and monitoring report for the Alaska park units (Redmond et al. 2005).

In climates that receive frozen precipitation, a decision must be made whether or not to try to record such events accurately. This usually means that the precipitation must be turned into liquid either by falling into an antifreeze fluid solution that is then weighed or by heating the precipitation enough to melt and fall through a measuring mechanism such as a nearly-balanced tipping bucket. Accurate measurements from the first approach require expensive gauges; tipping buckets can achieve this resolution readily but are more apt to lose some or all precipitation. Improvements have been made to the heating mechanism on the NWS tipping-bucket gauge used for the ASOS to correct its numerous deficiencies making it less problematic; however, this gauge is not inexpensive. A heat supply needed to melt frozen precipitation usually requires more energy than renewable energy (solar panels or wind recharging) can provide thus AC power is needed. Periods of frozen precipitation or rime often provide less-than-optimal recharging conditions with heavy clouds, short days, low-solar-elevation angles and more horizon blocking, and cold temperatures causing additional drain on the battery.

D.1.11. Save or Lose

A second consideration with precipitation is determining if the measurement should be saved (as in weighing systems) or lost (as in tipping-bucket systems). With tipping buckets, after the water has passed through the tipping mechanism, it usually just drops to the ground. Thus, there is no checksum to ensure that the sum of all the tips adds up to what has been saved in a reservoir at some location. By contrast, the weighing gauges continually accumulate until the reservoir is emptied, the reported value is the total reservoir content (for example, the height of the liquid column in a tube), and the incremental precipitation is the difference in depth between two known times. These weighing gauges do not always have the same fine resolution. Some gauges only record to the nearest centimeter, which is usually acceptable for hydrology but not necessarily for other needs. (For reference, a millimeter of precipitation can get a person in street clothes quite wet.) Other weighing gauges are capable of measuring to the 0.25-mm (0.01-in.) resolution but do not have as much capacity and must be emptied more often. Day/night and storm-related thermal expansion and contraction and sometimes wind shaking can cause fluid pressure from accumulated totals to go up and down in SNOTEL gauges by small increments (commonly 0.3-3 cm, or 0.01–0.10 ft) leading to "negative precipitation" followed by similarly non-real light precipitation when, in fact, no change took place in the amount of accumulated precipitation.

D.1.12. Time

Time should always be in local standard time (LST), and daylight savings time (DST) should never be used under any circumstances with automated equipment and timers. Using DST leads to one duplicate hour, one missing hour, and a season of displaced values, as well as needless confusion and a data-management nightmare. Absolute time, such as Greenwich Mean Time (GMT) or Coordinated Universal Time (UTC), also can be used because these formats are unambiguously translatable. Since measurements only provide information about what already *has* occurred or *is* occurring and not what *will* occur, they should always be assigned to the *ending time* of the associated interval with hour 24 marking the end of the last hour of the day. In this system, midnight always represents the end of the day, not the start. To demonstrate the importance of this differentiation, we have encountered situations where police officers seeking corroborating weather data could not recall whether the time on their crime report from a year ago was the starting midnight or the ending midnight! Station positions should be known to within a few meters, easily accomplished with GPS, so that time zones and solar angles can be determined accurately.

D.1.13. Automated versus Manual

Most of this report has addressed automated measurements. Historically, most measurements are manual and typically collected once a day. In many cases, manual measurements continue because of habit, usefulness, and desire for continuity over time. Manual measurements are extremely useful and when possible should be encouraged. However, automated measurements are becoming more common. For either, it is important to record time in a logically consistent manner.

It should not be automatically assumed that newer data and measurements are "better" than older data or that manual data are "worse" than automated data. Older or simpler manual measurements are often of very high quality even if they sometimes are not in the most convenient digital format.

There is widespread desire to use automated systems to reduce human involvement. This is admirable and understandable, but every automated weather/climate station or network requires significant human attention and maintenance. A telling example concerns the Oklahoma Mesonet (see Brock et al. 1995, and bibliography at http://www.mesonet.ou.edu), a network of about 115 high–quality, automated meteorological stations spread over Oklahoma, where about 80 percent of the annual ($2–3M) budget is nonetheless allocated to humans with only about 20 percent allocated to equipment.

D.1.14. Manual Conventions

Manual measurements typically are made once a day. Elements usually consist of maximum and minimum temperature, temperature at observation time, precipitation, snowfall, snow depth, and sometimes evaporation, wind, or other information. Since it is not actually known when extremes occurred, the only logical approach, and the nationwide convention, is to ascribe the entire measurement to the time-interval date and to enter it on the form in that way. For morning observers (for example, 8 am to 8 am), this means that the maximum temperature written for today often is from yesterday afternoon and sometimes the minimum temperature for the 24-hr period actually occurred yesterday morning. However, this is understood and expected. It is often a surprise to observers to see how many maximum temperatures do not occur in the afternoon and how many minimum temperatures do not occur in the predawn hours. This is especially true in environments that are colder, higher, northerly, cloudy, mountainous, or coastal. As long as this convention is strictly followed every day, it has been shown that truly excellent climate records can result (Redmond 1992). Manual observers should reset equipment only one time per day at the official observing time. Making more than one measurement a day is discouraged strongly; this practice results in a hybrid record that is too difficult to interpret. The only exception is for total daily snowfall. New snowfall can be measured up to four times per day with no observations closer than six hours. It is well known that more frequent measurement of snow increases the annual total because compaction is a continuous process.

Two main purposes for climate observations are to establish the long-term averages for given locations and to track variations in climate. Broadly speaking, these purposes address topics of absolute and relative climate behavior. Once absolute behavior has been "established" (a task that is never finished because long-term averages continue to vary in time)—temporal variability quickly becomes the item of most interest.

D.2. Representativeness

Having discussed important factors to consider when new sites are installed, we now turn our attention to site "representativeness." In popular usage, we often encounter the notion that a site is "representative" of another site if it receives the same annual precipitation or records the same annual temperature or if some other element-specific, long-term average has a similar value. This notion of representativeness has a certain limited validity, but there are other aspects of this idea that need to be considered.

A climate monitoring site also can be said to be representative if climate records from that site show sufficiently strong temporal correlations with a large number of locations over a sufficiently large area. If station A receives 20 cm a year and station B receives 200 cm a year, these climates obviously receive quite differing amounts of precipitation. However, if their monthly, seasonal, or annual correlations are high (for example, 0.80 or higher for a particular time scale), one site can be used as a surrogate for estimating values at the other if measurements for a particular month, season, or year are missing. That is, a wet or dry month at one station is also a wet or dry month (relative to its own mean) at the comparison station. Note that high correlations on one time scale do not imply automatically that high correlations will occur on other time scales.

Likewise, two stations having similar mean climates (for example, similar annual precipitation) might not co-vary in close synchrony (for example, coastal versus interior). This may be considered a matter of climate "affiliation" for a particular location.

Thus, the representativeness of a site can refer either to the basic climatic averages for a given duration (or time window within the annual cycle) or to the extent that the site co-varies in time with respect to all surrounding locations. One site can be representative of another in the first sense but not the second, or vice versa, or neither, or both—all combinations are possible.

If two sites are perfectly correlated then, in a sense, they are "redundant." However, redundancy has value because all sites will experience missing data especially with automated equipment in rugged environments and harsh climates where outages and other problems nearly can be guaranteed. In many cases, those outages are caused by the weather, particularly by unusual weather and the very conditions we most wish to know about. Methods for filling in those values will require proxy information from this or other nearby networks. Thus, redundancy is a virtue rather than a vice.

In general, the cooperative stations managed by the NWS have produced much longer records than automated stations like RAWS or SNOTEL stations. The RAWS stations often have problems with precipitation, especially in winter, or with missing data, so that low correlations may be data problems rather than climatic dissimilarity. The RAWS records also are relatively short, so correlations should be interpreted with care. In performing and interpreting such analyses, however, we must remember that there are physical climate reasons and observational reasons why stations within a short distance (even a few tens or hundreds of meters) may not correlate well.

D.2.1. Temporal Behavior

It is possible that high correlations will occur between station pairs during certain portions of the year (i.e., January) but low correlations may occur during other portions of the year (e.g., September or October). The relative contributions of these seasons to the annual total (for precipitation) or average (for temperature) and the correlations for each month are both factors in the correlation of an aggregated time window of longer duration that encompasses those seasons (e.g., one of the year definitions such as calendar year or water year). A complete and careful evaluation ideally would include such a correlation analysis but requires more resources and data. Note that it also is possible and frequently is observed that temperatures are highly correlated while precipitation is not or vice versa, and these relations can change according to the time of year. If two stations are well correlated for all climate elements for all portions of the year, then they can be considered redundant.

With scarce resources, the initial strategy should be to try to identify locations that do not correlate particularly well, so that each new site measures something new that cannot be guessed easily from the behavior of surrounding sites. (An important caveat here is that lack of such correlation could be a result of physical climate behavior and not a result of faults with the actual measuring process; i.e., by unrepresentative or simply poor-quality data. Unfortunately, we seldom have perfect climate data.) As additional sites are added, we usually wish for some combination of unique and redundant sites to meet the simultaneous needs for new information and more reliably-furnished information.

A common consideration is whether to observe on a ridge or in a valley, given the resources to place a single station within a particular area of a few square kilometers. Ridge and valley stations will correlate very well for temperatures when lapse conditions prevail, particularly summer daytime temperatures. In summer at night or winter at daylight, the picture will be more mixed and correlations will be lower. In winter at night when inversions are common and even the rule, correlations may be zero or even negative and perhaps even more divergent as the two sites are on opposite sides of the inversion. If we had the luxury of locating stations everywhere, we would find that ridge tops generally correlate very well with other ridge tops and similarly valleys with other valleys, but ridge tops correlate well with valleys only under certain circumstances. Beyond this, valleys and ridges having similar orientations usually will correlate better with each other than those with perpendicular orientations, depending on their orientation with respect to large-scale wind flow and solar angles.

Unfortunately, we do not have stations everywhere, so we are forced to use the few comparisons that we have and include a large dose of intelligent reasoning, using what we have observed elsewhere. In performing and interpreting such analyses, we must remember that there are physical climatic reasons and observational reasons why stations within a short distance (even a few tens or hundreds of meters) may not correlate well.

Examples of correlation analyses include those for the Channel Islands and for southwest Alaska, which can be found in Redmond and McCurdy (2005) and Redmond et al. (2005). These examples illustrate what can be learned from correlation analyses. Spatial correlations generally vary by time of year. Thus, results should be displayed in the form of annual correlation cycles—for monthly mean temperature and monthly total precipitation and perhaps other climate elements like wind or humidity—between station pairs selected for climatic setting and data availability and quality.

In general, the COOP stations managed by the NWS have produced much longer records than have automated stations like RAWS or SNOTEL stations. The RAWS stations also often have problems with precipitation, especially in winter or with missing data, so that low correlations may be data problems rather than climate dissimilarity. The RAWS records are much shorter, so correlations should be interpreted with care, but these stations are more likely to be in places of interest for remote or under-sampled regions.

D.2.2. Spatial Behavior
A number of techniques exist to interpolate from isolated point values to a spatial domain. For example, a common technique is simple inverse distance weighting. Critical to the success of the simplest of such techniques is that some other property of the spatial domain, one that is influential for the mapped element, does not vary significantly. Topography greatly influences precipitation, temperature, wind, humidity, and most other meteorological elements. Thus, this criterion clearly is not met in any region having extreme topographic diversity. In such circumstances, simple Cartesian distance may have little to do with how rapidly correlation deteriorates from one site to the next, and in fact, the correlations can decrease readily from a mountain to a valley and then increase again on the next mountain. Such structure in the fields of spatial correlation is not seen in the relatively (statistically) well-behaved flat areas like those in the eastern U.S.

To account for dominating effects such as topography and inland–coastal differences that exist in certain regions, some kind of additional knowledge must be brought to bear to produce meaningful, physically plausible, and observationally based interpolations. Historically, this has proven to be an extremely difficult problem, especially to perform objective and repeatable analyses. An analysis performed for southwest Alaska (Redmond et al. 2005) concluded that the PRISM (Parameter Regression on Independent Slopes Model) maps (Daly et al. 1994; 2002; Gibson et al. 2002; Doggett et al. 2004) were probably the best available. An analysis by Simpson et al. (2005) further discussed many issues in the mapping of Alaska's climate and resulted in the same conclusion about PRISM.

D.2.3. Climate-Change Detection
Although general purpose climate stations should be situated to address all aspects of climate variability, it is desirable that they also be in locations that are more sensitive to climate change from natural or anthropogenic influences should it begin to occur. The question here is how well

we know such sensitivities. The climate-change issue is quite complex because it encompasses more than just greenhouse gasses.

Sites that are in locations or climates particularly vulnerable to climate change should be favored. How this vulnerability is determined is a considerably challenging research issue. Candidate locations or situations are those that lie on the border between two major biomes or just inside the edge of one or the other. In these cases, a slight movement of the boundary in anticipated direction (toward "warmer," for example) would be much easier to detect as the boundary moves past the site and a different set of biota begin to be established. Such a vegetative or ecologic response would be more visible and would take less time to establish as a real change than would a smaller change in the center of the distribution range of a marker or key species.

D.2.4. Element-Specific Differences
The various climate elements (temperature, precipitation, cloudiness, snowfall, humidity, wind speed and direction, solar radiation) do not vary through time in the same sequence or manner nor should they necessarily be expected to vary in this manner. The spatial patterns of variability should not be expected to be the same for all elements. These patterns also should not be expected to be similar for all months or seasons. The suitability of individual sites for measurement also varies from one element to another. A site that has a favorable exposure for temperature or wind may not have a favorable exposure for precipitation or snowfall. A site that experiences proper air movement may be situated in a topographic channel, such as a river valley or a pass, which restricts the range of wind directions and affects the distribution of speed-direction categories.

D.2.5. Logistics and Practical Factors
Even with the most advanced scientific rationale, sites in some remote or climatically challenging settings may not be suitable because of the difficulty in servicing and maintaining equipment. Contributing to these challenges are scheduling difficulties, animal behavior, snow burial, icing, snow behavior, access and logistical problems, and the weather itself. Remote and elevated sites usually require far more attention and expense than a rain-dominated, easily accessible valley location.

For climate purposes, station exposure and the local environment should be maintained in their original state (vegetation especially), so that changes seen are the result of regional climate variations and not of trees growing up, bushes crowding a site, surface albedo changing, fire clearing, etc. Repeat photography has shown many examples of slow environmental change in the vicinity of a station in rather short time frames (5–20 years), and this technique should be employed routinely and frequently at all locations. In the end, logistics, maintenance, and other practical factors almost always determine the success of weather- and climate-monitoring activities.

D.2.6. Personnel Factors
Many past experiences (almost exclusively negative) strongly support the necessity to place primary responsibility for station deployment and maintenance in the hands of seasoned, highly qualified, trained, and meticulously careful personnel, the more experienced the better. Over

time, even in "benign" climates but especially where harsher conditions prevail, every conceivable problem will occur and both the usual and unusual should be anticipated: weather, animals, plants, salt, sensor and communication failure, windblown debris, corrosion, power failures, vibrations, avalanches, snow loading and creep, corruption of the data logger program, etc. An ability to anticipate and forestall such problems, a knack for innovation and improvisation, knowledge of electronics, practical and organizational skills, and presence of mind to bring the various small but vital parts, spares, tools, and diagnostic troubleshooting equipment are highly valued qualities. Especially when logistics are so expensive, a premium should be placed on using experienced personnel, since the slightest and seemingly most minor mistake can render a station useless or, even worse, uncertain. Exclusive reliance on individuals without this background can be costly and almost always will result eventually in unnecessary loss of data. Skilled labor and an apprenticeship system to develop new skilled labor will greatly reduce (but not eliminate) the types of problems that can occur in operating a climate network.

D.3. Site Selection
In addition to considerations identified previously in this appendix, various factors need to be considered in selecting sites for new or augmented instrumentation.

D.3.1. Equipment and Exposure Factors
D.3.1.1. Measurement Suite: All sites should measure temperature, humidity, wind, solar radiation, and snow depth. Precipitation measurements are more difficult but probably should be attempted with the understanding that winter measurements may be of limited or no value unless an all-weather gauge has been installed. Even if an all-weather gauge has been installed, it is desirable to have a second gauge present that operates on a different principle–for example, a fluid-based system like those used in the SNOTEL stations in tandem with a higher–resolution, tipping bucket gauge for summertime. Without heating, a tipping bucket gauge usually is of use only when temperatures are above freezing and when temperatures have not been below freezing for some time, so that accumulated ice and snow is not melting and being recorded as present precipitation. Gauge undercatch is a significant issue in snowy climates, so shielding should be considered for all gauges designed to work over the winter months. It is very important to note the presence or absence of shielding, the type of shielding, and the dates of installation or removal of the shielding.

D.3.1.2. Overall Exposure: The ideal, general all-purpose site has gentle slopes, is open to the sun and the wind, has a natural vegetative cover, avoids strong local (less than 200 m) influences, and represents a reasonable compromise among all climate elements. The best temperature sites are not the best precipitation sites, and the same is true for other elements. Steep topography in the immediate vicinity should be avoided unless settings where precipitation is affected by steep topography are being deliberately sought or a mountaintop or ridgeline is the desired location. The potential for disturbance should be considered: fire and flood risk, earth movement, wind-borne debris, volcanic deposits or lahars, vandalism, animal tampering, and general human encroachment are all factors.

D.3.1.3. Elevation: Mountain climates do not vary in time in exactly the same manner as adjoining valley climates. This concept is emphasized when temperature inversions are present to a greater degree and during precipitation when winds rise up the slopes at the same angle.

There is considerable concern that mountain climates will be (or already are) changing and perhaps changing differently than lowland climates, which has direct and indirect consequences for plant and animal life in the more extreme zones. Elevations of special significance are those that are near the mean rain/snow line for winter, near the tree line, and near the mean annual freezing level (all of these may not be quite the same). Because the lapse rates in wet climates often are nearly moist-adiabatic during the main precipitation seasons, measurements at one elevation may be extrapolated to nearby elevations. In drier climates and in the winter, temperature and to a lesser extent wind will show various elevation profiles.

D.3.1.4. Transects: The concept of observing transects that span climatic gradients is sound. This is not always straightforward in topographically uneven terrain, but these transects could still be arranged by setting up station(s) along the coast; in or near passes atop the main coastal interior drainage divide; and inland at one, two, or three distances into the interior lowlands. Transects need not—and by dint of topographic constraints probably cannot—be straight lines, but the closer that a line can be approximated the better. The main point is to systematically sample the key points of a behavioral transition without deviating too radically from linearity.

D.3.1.5. Other Topographic Considerations: There are various considerations with respect to local topography. Local topography can influence wind (channeling, upslope/downslope, etc.), precipitation (orographic enhancement, downslope evaporation, catch efficiency, etc.), and temperature (frost pockets, hilltops, aspect, mixing or decoupling from the overlying atmosphere, bowls, radiative effects, etc.), to different degrees at differing scales. In general, for measurements to be areally representative, it is better to avoid these local effects to the extent that they can be identified before station deployment (once deployed, it is desirable not to move a station). The primary purpose of a climate-monitoring network should be to serve as an infrastructure in the form of a set of benchmark stations for comparing other stations. Sometimes, however, it is exactly these local phenomena that we want to capture. Living organisms, especially plants, are affected by their immediate environment, whether it is representative of a larger setting or not. Specific measurements of limited scope and duration made for these purposes then can be tied to the main benchmarks. This experience is useful also in determining the complexity needed in the benchmark monitoring process in order to capture particular phenomena at particular space and time scales.

Sites that drain (cold air) well generally are better than sites that allow cold air to pool. Slightly sloped areas (1 degree is fine) or small benches from tens to hundreds of meters above streams are often favorable locations. Furthermore, these sites often tend to be out of the path of hazards (like floods) and to have rocky outcroppings where controlling vegetation will not be a major concern. Benches or wide spots on the rise between two forks of a river system are often the only flat areas and sometimes jut out to give greater exposure to winds from more directions.

D.3.1.6. Prior History: The starting point in designing a program is to determine what kinds of observations have been collected over time, by whom, in what manner, and if these observation are continuing to the present time. It also may be of value to "re-occupy" the former site of a station that is now inactive to provide some measure of continuity or a reference point from the past. This can be of value even if continuous observations were not made during the entire intervening period.

D.3.2. Element-Specific Factors

D.3.2.1. Temperature: An open exposure with uninhibited air movement is the preferred setting. The most common measurement is made at approximately eye level, 1.5–2.0 m. In snowy locations sensors should be at least one meter higher than the deepest snowpack expected in the next 50 years or perhaps 2–3 times the depth of the average maximum annual depth. Sensors should be shielded above and below from solar radiation (bouncing off snow), from sunrise/sunset horizontal input, and from vertical rock faces. Sensors should be clamped tightly, so that they do not swivel away from level stacks of radiation plates. Nearby vegetation should be kept away from the sensors (several meters). Growing vegetation should be cut to original conditions. Small hollows and swales can cool tremendously at night, and it is best avoid these areas. Side slopes of perhaps a degree or two of angle facilitate air movement and drainage and, in effect, sample a large area during nighttime hours. The very bottom of a valley should be avoided. Temperature can change substantially from moves of only a few meters. Situations have been observed where flat and seemingly uniform conditions (like airport runways) appear to demonstrate different climate behaviors over short distances of a few tens or hundreds of meters (differences of 5–10°C). When snow is on the ground, these microclimatic differences can be stronger, and differences of 2–5°C can occur in the short distance between the thermometer and the snow surface on calm evenings.

D.3.2.2. Precipitation (liquid): Calm locations with vegetative or artificial shielding are preferred. Wind will adversely impact readings; therefore, the less the better. Wind effects on precipitation are far less for rain than for snow. Devices that "save" precipitation present advantages, but most gauges are built to dump precipitation as it falls or to empty periodically. Automated gauges give both the amount and the timing. Simple backups that record only the total precipitation since the last visit have a certain advantage (for example, storage gauges or lengths of PVC pipe perhaps with bladders on the bottom). The following question should be asked: Does the total precipitation from an automated gauge add up to the measured total in a simple bucket (evaporation is prevented with an appropriate substance such as mineral oil)? Drip from overhanging foliage and trees can augment precipitation totals.

D.3.2.3. Precipitation (frozen): Calm locations or shielding are a must. Undercatch for rain is only about 5 percent, but with winds of only 2–4 m/s, gauges may catch only 30–70 percent of the actual snow falling depending on density of the flakes. To catch 100 percent of the snow, the standard configuration for shielding is employed by the CRN (Climate Reference Network): the DFIR (Double-Fence Intercomparison Reference) shield with 2.4-m (8-ft.) vertical, wooden slatted fences in two concentric octagons with diameters of 8 m and 4 m (26 ft and 13 ft, respectively) and an inner Alter shield (flapping vanes). Numerous tests have shown this is the only way to achieve complete catch of snowfall (e.g., Yang et al. 1998; 2001). The DFIR shield is large and bulky; it is recommended that all precipitation gauges have at least Alter shields on them.

Near oceans, much snow is heavy and falls more vertically. In colder locations or storms, light flakes frequently will fly in and then out of the gauge. Clearings in forests are usually excellent sites. Snow blowing from trees that are too close can augment actual precipitation totals. Artificial shielding (vanes, etc.) placed around gauges in snowy locales always should be used if accurate totals are desired. Moving parts tend to freeze up. Capping of gauges during heavy snowfall events is a common occurrence. When the cap becomes pointed, snow falls off to the ground and is not recorded. Caps and plugs often will not fall into the tube until hours, days, or even weeks have passed, typically during an extended period of freezing temperature or above or when sunlight finally occurs. Liquid-based measurements (e.g., SNOTEL "rocket" gauges) do not have the resolution (usually 0.3 cm [0.1 in.] rather than 0.03 cm [0.01 in.]) that tipping bucket and other gauges have but are known to be reasonably accurate in very snowy climates. Light snowfall events might not be recorded until enough of them add up to the next reporting increment. More expensive gauges like Geonors can be considered and could do quite well in snowy settings; however, they need to be emptied every 40 cm (15 in.) or so (capacity of 51 cm [20 in.]) until the new 91-cm (36-in.) capacity gauge is offered for sale. Recently, the NWS has been trying out the new (and very expensive) Ott all-weather gauge. Riming can be an issue in windy foggy environments below freezing. Rime, dew, and other forms of atmospheric condensation are not real precipitation, since they are caused by the gauge.

D.3.2.4. Snow Depth: Windswept areas tend to be blown clear of snow. Conversely, certain types of vegetation can act as a snow fence and cause artificial drifts. However, some amount of vegetation in the vicinity generally can help slow down the wind. The two most common types of snow-depth gauges are the Judd Snow Depth Sensor, produced by Judd Communications, and the snow depth gauge produced by Campbell Scientific, Inc. Opinions vary on which one is better. These gauges use ultrasound and look downward in a cone about 22 degrees in diameter. The ground should be relatively clear of vegetation and maintained in a manner so that the zero point on the calibration scale does not change.

D.3.2.5. Snow Water Equivalent: This is determined by the weight of snow on fluid-filled pads about the size of a desktop set up sometimes in groups of four or in larger hexagons several meters in diameter. These pads require flat ground some distance from nearby sources of windblown snow and shielding that is "just right": not too close to the shielding to act as a kind of snow fence and not too far from the shielding so that blowing and drifting become a factor. Generally, these pads require fluids that possess antifreeze-like properties, as well as handling and replacement protocols.

D.3.2.6. Wind: Open exposures are needed for wind measurements. Small prominences or benches without blockage from certain sectors are preferred. A typical rule for trees is to site stations back 10 tree-heights from all tree obstructions. Sites in long, narrow valleys can obviously only exhibit two main wind directions. Gently rounded eminences are more favored. Any kind of topographic steering should be avoided to the extent possible. Avoiding major mountain chains or single isolated mountains or ridges is usually a favorable approach, if there is a choice. Sustained wind speed and the highest gusts (1-second) should be recorded. Averaging methodologies for both sustained winds and gusts can affect climate trends and should be recorded as metadata with all changes noted. Vegetation growth affects the vertical wind profile, and growth over a few years can lead to changes in mean wind speed even if the "real" wind does not change, so vegetation near the site (perhaps out to 50 m) should be maintained in a quasi-permanent status (same height and spatial distribution). Wind devices can rime up and freeze or spin out of balance. In severely rimed or windy climates, rugged anemometers, such as those made by Taylor, are worth considering. These anemometers are expensive but durable and can withstand substantial abuse. In exposed locations, personnel should plan for winds to be at least 50 m/s and be able to measure these wind speeds. At a minimum, anemometers should be rated to 75 m/s.

D.3.2.7. Humidity: Humidity is a relatively straightforward climate element. Close proximity to lakes or other water features can affect readings. Humidity readings typically are less accurate near 100 percent and at low humidities in cold weather.

D.3.2.8. Solar Radiation: A site with an unobstructed horizon obviously is the most desirable. This generally implies a flat plateau or summit. However, in most locations trees or mountains will obstruct the sun for part of the day.

D.3.2.9. Soil Temperature: It is desirable to measure soil temperature at locations where soil is present. If soil temperature is recorded at only a single depth, the most preferred depth is 10 cm. Other common depths include 25 cm, 50 cm, 2 cm, and 100 cm. Biological activity in the soil will be proportional to temperature with important threshold effects occurring near freezing.

D.3.2.10. Soil Moisture: Soil-moisture gauges are somewhat temperamental and require care to install. The soil should be characterized by a soil expert during installation of the gauge. The readings may require a certain level of experience to interpret correctly. If accurate, readings of soil moisture are especially useful.

D.3.2.11. Distributed Observations: It can be seen readily that compromises must be struck among the considerations described in the preceding paragraphs because some are mutually exclusive.

How large can a "site" be? Generally, the equipment footprint should be kept as small as practical with all components placed next to each other (within less than 10–20 m or so). Readings from one instrument frequently are used to aid in interpreting readings from the remaining instruments.

What is a tolerable degree of separation? Some consideration may be given to locating a precipitation gauge or snow pillow among protective vegetation, while the associated temperature, wind, and humidity readings would be collected more effectively in an open and exposed location within 20–50 m. Ideally, it is advantageous to know the wind measurement precisely at the precipitation gauge, but a compromise involving a short split, and in effect a "distributed observation," could be considered. There are no definitive rules governing this decision, but it is suggested that the site footprint be kept within approximately 50 m. There also are constraints imposed by engineering and electrical factors that affect cable lengths, signal strength, and line noise; therefore, the shorter the cable the better. Practical issues include the need to trench a channel to outlying instruments or to allow lines to lie atop the ground and associated problems with animals, humans, weathering, etc. Separating a precipitation gauge up to 100 m or so from an instrument mast may be an acceptable compromise if other factors are not limiting.

D.3.2.12. Instrument Replacement Schedules: Instruments slowly degrade, and a plan for replacing them with new, refurbished, or recalibrated instruments should be in place. After approximately five years, a systematic change-out procedure should result in replacing most sensors in a network. Certain parts, such as solar radiation sensors, are candidates for annual calibration or change-out. Anemometers tend to degrade as bearings erode or electrical contacts become uneven. Noisy bearings are an indication, and a stethoscope might aid in hearing such noises. Increased internal friction affects the threshold starting speed; once spinning, they tend to function properly. Increases in starting threshold speeds can lead to more zero-wind measurements and thus reduce the reported mean wind speed with no real change in wind properties. A field calibration kit should be developed and taken on all site visits, routine or otherwise. Rain gauges can be tested with drip testers during field visits. Protective conduit and tight water seals can prevent abrasion and moisture problems with the equipment, although seals can keep moisture in as well as out. Bulletproof casings sometimes are employed in remote settings. A supply of spare parts, at least one of each and more for less-expensive or more-delicate sensors, should be maintained to allow replacement of worn or nonfunctional instruments during field visits. In addition, this approach allows instruments to be calibrated in the relative convenience of the operational home—the larger the network, the greater the need for a parts depot.

D.3.3. Long-Term Comparability and Consistency

D.3.3.1. Consistency: The emphasis here is to hold biases constant. Every site has biases, problems, and idiosyncrasies of one sort or another. The best rule to follow is simply to try to keep biases constant through time. Since the goal is to track climate through time, keeping sensors, methodologies, and exposure constant will ensure that only true climate change is being measured. This means leaving the site in its original state or performing maintenance to keep it that way. Once a site is installed, the goal should be to never move the site even by a few meters or to allow significant changes to occur within 100 m for the next several decades.

Sites in or near rock outcroppings likely will experience less vegetative disturbance or growth through the years and will not usually retain moisture, a factor that could speed corrosion. Sites that will remain locally similar for some time are usually preferable. However, in some cases the intent of a station might be to record the local climate effects of changes within a small-scale system (for example, glacier, recently burned area, or scene of some other disturbance) that is subject to a regional climate influence. In this example, the local changes might be much larger than the regional changes.

D.3.3.2. Metadata: Since the climate of every site is affected by features in the immediate vicinity, it is vital to record this information over time and to update the record repeatedly at each service visit. Distances, angles, heights of vegetation, fine-scale topography, condition of instruments, shielding discoloration, and other factors from within a meter to several kilometers should be noted. Systematic photography should be undertaken and updated at least once every one–two years.

Photographic documentation should be taken at each site in a standard manner and repeated every two–three years. Guidelines for methodology were developed by Redmond (2004) as a result of experience with the NOAA CRN and can be found on the WRCC NPS Web pages at http://www.wrcc.dri.edu/nps and at ftp://ftp.wrcc.dri.edu/nps/photodocumentation.pdf.

The main purpose for climate stations is to *track climatic conditions through time*. Anything that affects the interpretation of records through time must to be noted and recorded for posterity. The important factors should be clear to a person who has never visited the site, no matter how long ago the site was installed.

In regions with significant, climatic transition zones, transects are an efficient way to span several climates and make use of available resources. Discussions on this topic at greater detail can be found in Redmond and Simeral (2004) and in Redmond et al. (2005).

D.4. Literature Cited

American Association of State Climatologists. 1985. Heights and exposure standards for sensors on automated weather stations. The State Climatologist **9**.

Brock, F. V., K. C. Crawford, R. L. Elliott, G. W. Cuperus, S. J. Stadler, H. L. Johnson and M. D. Eilts. 1995. The Oklahoma Mesonet: A technical overview. Journal of Atmospheric and Oceanic Technology **12**:5-19.

Daly, C., R. P. Neilson, and D. L. Phillips. 1994. A statistical-topographic model for mapping climatological precipitation over mountainous terrain. Journal of Applied Meteorology **33**:140-158.

Daly, C., W. P. Gibson, G. H. Taylor, G. L. Johnson, and P. Pasteris. 2002. A knowledge-based approach to the statistical mapping of climate. Climate Research **22**:99-113.

Doggett, M., C. Daly, J. Smith, W. Gibson, G. Taylor, G. Johnson, and P. Pasteris. 2004. High-resolution 1971-2000 mean monthly temperature maps for the western United States. Fourteenth AMS Conf. on Applied Climatology, 84th AMS Annual Meeting. Seattle, WA, American Meteorological Society, Boston, MA, January 2004, Paper 4.3, CD-ROM.

Geiger, R., R. H. Aron, and P. E. Todhunter. 2003. The Climate Near the Ground. 6th edition. Rowman & Littlefield Publishers, Inc., New York.

Gibson, W. P., C. Daly, T. Kittel, D. Nychka, C. Johns, N. Rosenbloom, A. McNab, and G. Taylor. 2002. Development of a 103-year high-resolution climate data set for the conterminous United States. Thirteenth AMS Conf. on Applied Climatology. Portland, OR, American Meteorological Society, Boston, MA, May 2002:181-183.

Goodison, B. E., P. Y. T. Louie, and D. Yang. 1998. WMO solid precipitation measurement intercomparison final report. WMO TD 982, World Meteorological Organization, Geneva, Switzerland.

National Research Council. 1998. Future of the National Weather Service Cooperative Weather Network. National Academies Press, Washington, D.C.

National Research Council. 2001. A Climate Services Vision: First Steps Toward the Future. National Academies Press, Washington, D.C.

Redmond, K. T. 1992. Effects of observation time on interpretation of climatic time series - A need for consistency. Eighth Annual Pacific Climate (PACLIM) Workshop. Pacific Grove, CA, March 1991:141-150.

Redmond, K. T. 2004. Photographic documentation of long-term climate stations. Available from ftp://ftp.wrcc.dri.edu/nps/photodocumentation.pdf. (accessed 15 August 2004)

Redmond, K. T. and D. B. Simeral. 2004. Climate monitoring comments: Central Alaska Network Inventory and Monitoring Program. Available from ftp://ftp.wrcc.dri.edu/nps/alaska/cakn/npscakncomments040406.pdf. (accessed 6 April 2004)

Redmond, K. T., D. B. Simeral, and G. D. McCurdy. 2005. Climate monitoring for southwest Alaska national parks: network design and site selection. Report 05-01. Western Regional Climate Center, Reno, Nevada.

Redmond, K. T., and G. D. McCurdy. 2005. Channel Islands National Park: Design considerations for weather and climate monitoring. Report 05-02. Western Regional Climate Center, Reno, Nevada.

Sevruk, B., and W. R. Hamon. 1984. International comparison of national precipitation gauges with a reference pit gauge. Instruments and Observing Methods, Report No 17, WMO/TD – 38, World Meteorological Organization, Geneva, Switzerland.

Simpson, J. J., Hufford, G. L., C. Daly, J. S. Berg, and M. D. Fleming. 2005. Comparing maps of mean monthly surface temperature and precipitation for Alaska and adjacent areas of Canada produced by two different methods. Arctic **58**:137-161.

Whiteman, C. D. 2000. Mountain Meteorology: Fundamentals and Applications. Oxford University Press, Oxford, UK.

Wilson, E. O. 1998. Consilience: The Unity of Knowledge. Knopf, New York.

World Meteorological Organization. 1983. Guide to meteorological instruments and methods of observation, No. 8, 5th edition, World Meteorological Organization, Geneva Switzerland.

World Meteorological Organization. 2005. Organization and planning of intercomparisons of rainfall intensity gauges. World Meteorological Organization, Geneva Switzerland.

Yang, D., B. E. Goodison, J. R. Metcalfe, V. S. Golubev, R. Bates, T. Pangburn, and C. Hanson. 1998. Accuracy of NWS 8" standard nonrecording precipitation gauge: results and application of WMO intercomparison. Journal of Atmospheric and Oceanic Technology **15**:54-68.

Yang, D., B. E. Goodison, J. R. Metcalfe, P. Louie, E. Elomaa, C. Hanson, V. Bolubev, T. Gunther, J. Milkovic, and M. Lapin. 2001. Compatibility evaluation of national precipitation gauge measurements. Journal of Geophysical Research **106**:1481-1491.

Appendix E. Master metadata field list

Field Name	Field Type	Field Description
begin_date	date	Effective beginning date for a record.
begin_date_flag	char(2)	Flag describing the known accuracy of the begin date for a station.
best_elevation	float(4)	Best known elevation for a station (in feet).
clim_div_code	char(2)	Foreign key defining climate division code (primary in table: clim_div).
clim_div_key	int2	Foreign key defining climate division for a station (primary in table: clim_div.
clim_div_name	varchar(30)	English name for a climate division.
controller_info	varchar(50)	Person or organization who maintains the identifier system for a given weather or climate network.
country_key	int2	Foreign key defining country where a station resides (primary in table: none).
county_key	int2	Foreign key defining county where a station resides (primary in table: county).
county_name	varchar(31)	English name for a county.
description	text	Any description pertaining to the particular table.
end_date	date	Last effective date for a record.
end_date_flag	char(2)	Flag describing the known accuracy of station end date.
fips_country_code	char(2)	FIPS (federal information processing standards) country code.
fips_state_abbr	char(2)	FIPS state abbreviation for a station.
fips_state_code	char(2)	FIPS state code for a station.
history_flag	char(2)	Describes temporal significance of an individual record among others from the same station.
id_type_key	int2	Foreign key defining the id_type for a station (usually defined in code).
last_updated	date	Date of last update for a record.
latitude	float(8)	Latitude value.
longitude	float(8)	Longitude value.
name_type_key	int2	"3": COOP station name, "2": best station name.
name	varchar(30)	Station name as known at date of last update entry.
ncdc_state_code	char(2)	NCDC, two-character code identifying U.S. state.
network_code	char(8)	Eight-character abbreviation code identifying a network.
network_key	int2	Foreign key defining the network for a station (primary in table: network).
network_station_id	int4	Identifier for a station in the associated network, which is defined by id_type_key.
remark	varchar(254)	Additional information for a record.
src_quality_code	char(2)	Code describing the data quality for the data source.
state_key	int2	Foreign key defining the U.S. state where a station resides (primary in table: state).
state_name	varchar(30)	English name for a state.
station_alt_name	varchar(30)	Other English names for a station.
station_best_name	varchar(30)	Best, most well-known English name for a station.
time_zone	float4	Time zone where a station resides.
ucan_station_id	int4	Unique station identifier for every station in ACIS.
unit_key	int2	Integer value representing a unit of measure.

Field Name	Field Type	Field Description
updated_by	char(8)	Person who last updated a record.
var_major_id	int2	Defines major climate variable.
var_minor_id	int2	Defines data source within a var_major_id.
zipcode	char(5)	Zipcode where a latitude/longitude point resides.
nps_netcode	char(4)	Network four-character identifier.
nps_netname	varchar(128)	Displayed English name for a network.
parkcode	char(4)	Park four-character identifier.
parkname	varchar(128)	Displayed English name for a park/
im_network	char(4)	NPS I&M network where park belongs (a net code)/
station_id	varchar(16)	Station identifier.
station_id_type	varchar(16)	Type of station identifier.
network.subnetwork.id	varchar(16)	Identifier of a sub-network in associated network.
subnetwork_key	int2	Foreign key defining sub-network for a station.
subnetwork_name	varchar(30)	English name for a sub-network.
slope	integer	Terrain slope at the location.
aspect	integer	Terrain aspect at the station.
gps	char(1)	Indicator of latitude/longitude recorded via GPS.
site_description	text(0)	Physical description of site.
route_directions	text(0)	Driving route or site access directions.
station_photo_id	integer	Unique identifier associating a group of photos to a station. Group of photos all taken on same date.
photo_id	char(30)	Unique identifier for a photo.
photo_date	datetime	Date photograph taken.
photographer	varchar(64)	Name of photographer.
maintenance_date	datetime	Date of station maintenance visit.
contact_key	Integer	Unique identifier associating contact information to a station.
full_name	varchar(64)	Full name of contact person.
organization	varchar(64)	Organization of contact person.
contact_type	varchar(32)	Type of contact person (operator, administrator, etc.)
position_title	varchar(32)	Title of contact person.
address	varchar(32)	Address for contact person.
city	varchar(32)	City for contact person.
state	varchar(2)	State for contact person.
zip_code	char(10)	Zipcode for contact person.
country	varchar(32)	Country for contact person.
email	varchar(64)	E-mail for contact person.
work_phone	varchar(16)	Work phone for contact person.
contact_notes	text(254)	Other details regarding contact person.
equipment_type	char(30)	Sensor measurement type; i.e., wind speed, air temperature, etc.
eq_manufacturer	char(30)	Manufacturer of equipment.
eq_model	char(20)	Model number of equipment.
serial_num	char(20)	Serial number of equipment.
eq_description	varchar(254)	Description of equipment.
install_date	datetime	Installation date of equipment.
remove_date	datetime	Removal date of equipment.
ref_height	integer	Sensor displacement height from surface.
sampling_interval	varchar(10)	Frequency of sensor measurement.

Appendix F. Electronic supplements

F.1. ACIS metadata file for weather and climate stations associated with the NGPN:
http://www.wrcc.dri.edu/nps/pub/NGPN/metadata/NGPN_from_ACIS.tar.gz.

F.2. NGPN metadata files for weather and climate stations associated with the NGPN:
http://www.wrcc.dri.edu/nps/pub/NGPN/metadata/NGPN_NPS.tar.gz.

Appendix G. Descriptions of weather/climate monitoring networks

G.1. Automated Weather Data Network (AWDN)

- Purpose of network: provide denser coverage of near-real-time weather data for the Great Plains.
- Primary management agency: HPRCC.
- Data website: http://www.hprcc.unl.edu/awdn.
- Measured weather/climate elements:
  o Air temperature.
  o Relative humidity.
  o Precipitation.
  o Wind.
  o Solar radiation.
- Sampling frequency: hourly.
- Reporting frequency: hourly.
- Estimated station cost: unknown.
- Network strengths:
  o Network has near-real-time data.
  o Coverage is extensive across the northern Great Plains.
- Network weaknesses:
  o Maintenance and data quality are uncertain.

The AWDN is operated by HPRCC and was initiated to provide denser coverage of near-real-time weather data for the Great Plains. Hourly data are recorded for air temperature and humidity, wind speed and direction, solar radiation, and precipitation.

G.2. Clean Air Status and Trends Network (CASTNet)

- Purpose of network: provide information for evaluating the effectiveness of national emission-control strategies.
- Primary management agency: EPA.
- Data website: http://epa.gov/castnet/.
- Measured weather/climate elements:
  o Air temperature.
  o Precipitation.
  o Relative humidity.
  o Wind speed.
  o Wind direction.
  o Wind gust.
  o Gust direction.
  o Solar radiation.
  o Soil moisture and temperature.
- Sampling frequency: hourly.
- Reporting frequency: hourly.

- Estimated station cost: $13000.
- Network strengths:
  - High-quality data.
  - Sites are well maintained.
- Network weaknesses:
  - Density of station coverage is low.
  - Shorter periods of record for western U.S.

The CASTNet network is primarily is an air-quality-monitoring network managed by the EPA. The elements shown here are intended to support interpretation of measured air-quality parameters such as ozone, nitrates, sulfides, etc., which also are measured at CASTNet sites.

G.3. NWS Cooperative Observer Program (COOP)

- Purpose of network:
  - Provide observational, meteorological data required to define U.S. climate and help measure long-term climate changes.
  - Provide observational, meteorological data in near real-time to support forecasting and warning mechanisms and other public service programs of the NWS.
- Primary management agency: NOAA (NWS).
- Data website: data are available from the NCDC (http://www.ncdc.noaa.gov), RCCs (e.g., WRCC, http://www.wrcc.dri.edu), and state climate offices.
- Measured weather/climate elements:
  - Maximum, minimum, and observation-time temperature.
  - Precipitation, snowfall, snow depth.
  - Pan evaporation (some stations).
- Sampling frequency: daily.
- Reporting frequency: daily or monthly (station-dependent).
- Estimated station cost: $2000 with maintenance costs of $500–900/year.
- Network strengths:
  - Decade–century records at most sites.
  - Widespread national coverage (thousands of stations).
  - Excellent data quality when well maintained.
  - Relatively inexpensive; highly cost effective.
  - Manual measurements; not automated.
- Network weaknesses:
  - Uneven exposures; many are not well-maintained.
  - Dependence on schedules for volunteer observers.
  - Slow entry of data from many stations into national archives.
  - Data subject to observational methodology; not always documented.
  - Manual measurements; not automated and not hourly.

The COOP network has long served as the main climate observation network in the U.S. Readings are usually made by volunteers using equipment supplied, installed, and maintained by the federal government. The observer in effect acts as a host for the data-gathering activities and supplies the labor; this is truly a "cooperative" effort. The SAO sites often are considered to be part of the cooperative network as well if they collect the previously mentioned types of weather/climate observations. Typical observation days are morning to morning, evening to evening, or midnight to midnight. By convention, observations are ascribed to the date the instrument was reset at the end of the observational period. For this reason, midnight observations represent the end of a day. The Historical Climate Network is a subset of the cooperative network but contains longer and more complete records.

G.4. NOAA Climate Reference Network (CRN)

- Purpose of network: provide long-term homogeneous measurements of temperature and precipitation that can be coupled with long-term historic observations to monitor present and future climate change.
- Primary management agency: NOAA.
- Data website: http://www.ncdc.noaa.gov/crn/.
- Measured weather/climate elements:
  o Air temperature (triply redundant, aspirated).
  o Precipitation (three-wire Geonor gauge).
  o Wind speed.
  o Solar radiation.
  o Ground surface temperature.
- Sampling frequency: precipitation can be sampled either 5 or 15 minutes. Temperature sampled every 5 minutes. All other elements sampled every 15 minutes.
- Reporting frequency: hourly or every three hours.
- Estimated station cost: $30000, with maintenance costs around $2000/year.
- Network strengths:
  o Station siting is excellent (appropriate for long-term climate monitoring).
  o Data quality is excellent.
  o Site maintenance is excellent.
- Network weaknesses:
  o CRN network is still developing.
  o Station coverage is limited.
  o Not intended for snowy climates.

Data from the CRN are used in operational climate-monitoring activities and are used to place current climate patterns into a historic perspective. The CRN is intended as a reference network for the U.S. that meets the requirements of the Global Climate Observing System. Up to 115 CRN sites are planned for installation, but the actual number of installed sites will depend on available funding.

G.5. Citizen Weather Observer Program (CWOP)

- Purpose of network: collect observations from private citizens and make these data available for homeland security and other weather applications, providing constant feedback to the observers to maintain high data quality.
- Primary management agency: NOAA MADIS program.
- Data Website: http://www.wxqa.com.
- Measured weather/climate elements:

o Air temperature.
o Dewpoint temperature.
o Precipitation.
o Wind speed and direction.
o Barometric pressure.
- Sampling frequency: 15 minutes or less.
- Reporting frequency: 15 minutes.
- Estimated station cost: unknown.
- Network strengths:
  o Active partnership between public agencies and private citizens.
  o Large number of participant sites.
  o Regular communications between data providers and users, encouraging higher data quality.
- Network weaknesses:
  o Variable instrumentation platforms.
  o Metadata are sometimes limited.

The CWOP network is a public-private partnership with U.S. citizens and various agencies including NOAA, NASA (National Aeronautics and Space Administration), and various universities. There are over 4500 registered sites worldwide, with close to 3000 of these sites located in North America.

G.6. NPS Gaseous Pollutant Monitoring Program (GPMP)

- Purpose of network: measurement of ozone and related meteorological elements.
- Primary management agency: NPS.
- Data website: http://www2.nature.nps.gov/air/monitoring.
- Measured weather/climate elements:
  o Air temperature.
  o Relative humidity.
  o Precipitation.
  o Wind speed and direction.
  o Solar radiation.
  o Surface wetness.
- Sampling frequency: continuous.
- Reporting frequency: hourly.
- Estimated station cost: unknown.
- Network strengths:
  o Stations are located within NPS park units.
  o Data quality is excellent, with high data standards.
  o Provides unique measurements that are not available elsewhere.
  o Records are up to 2 decades in length.
  o Site maintenance is excellent.
  o Thermometers are aspirated.
- Network weaknesses:
  o Not easy to download the entire data set or to ingest live data.

o Station spacing and coverage: station installation is episodic, driven by opportunistic situations.

The NPS web site indicates that there are 33 sites with continuous ozone analysis run by NPS, with records from a few to about 16-17 years. Of these stations, 12 are labeled as GPMP sites and the rest are labeled as CASTNet sites. All of these have standard meteorological measurements, including a 10-m mast. Another nine GPMP sites are located within NPS units but run by cooperating agencies. A number of other sites (1-2 dozen) ran for differing periods in the past, generally less than 5-10 years.

G.7. NOAA Ground-Based GPS Meteorology (GPS-MET) Network

- Purpose of network:
  - o Measure atmospheric water vapor using ground-based GPS receivers.
  - o Facilitate use of these data operational and in other research and applications.
  - o Provides data for weather forecasting, atmospheric modeling and prediction, climate monitoring, calibrating and validation other observing systems including radiosondes and satellites, and research.
- Primary management agency: NOAA Earth System Research Laboratory.
- Data website: http://gpsmet.noaa.gov/jsp/index.jsp.
- Measurements:
  - o Dual frequency carrier phase measurements every 30 seconds.
- Ancillary weather/climate observations:
  - o Air temperature.
  - o Relative humidity.
  - o Barometric pressure.
- Reporting frequency: currently 30 min.
- Estimated station cost: $0-$10000, depending on approach. Data from dual frequency GPS receivers installed for conventional applications (e.g., high accuracy surveying) can be used without modification.
- Network strengths:
  - o Frequent, high-quality measurements.
  - o High reliability.
  - o All-weather operability.
  - o Many uses.
  - o Highly leveraged.
  - o Requires no calibration.
  - o Measurement accuracy improves with time.
- Network weakness:
  - o Point measurement.
  - o Provides no direct information about the vertical distribution of water vapor.

The GPS-MET network is the first network of its kind dedicated to GPS meteorology (see Duan et al. 1996). The GPS-MET network was developed in response to the need for improved moisture observations to support weather forecasting, climate monitoring, and other research activities. GPS-MET is a collaboration between NOAA and several other governmental and university organizations and institutions.

GPS meteorology utilizes the radio signals broadcast by the satellite Global Positioning System for atmospheric remote sensing. GPS meteorology applications have evolved along two paths: ground-based (Bevis et al. 1992) and space-based (Yuan et al. 1993). Both applications make the same fundamental measurement (the apparent delay in the arrival of radio signals caused by changes in the radio-refractivity of the atmosphere along the paths of the radio signals) but they do so from different perspectives.

In ground-based GPS meteorology, a GPS receiver and antenna are placed at a fixed location on the ground and the signals from all GPS satellites in view are continuously recorded. From this information, the exact position of the GPS antenna can be determined over time with high (millimeter-level) accuracy. Subsequent measurements of the antenna position are compared with the known position, and the differences can be attributed to changes in the temperature, pressure and water vapor in the atmosphere above the antenna. By making continuous measurements of temperature and pressure at the site, the total amount of water vapor in the atmosphere at this location can be estimated with high accuracy under all weather conditions. For more information on ground based GPS meteorology the reader is referred to http://gpsmet.noaa.gov.

In space-based GPS meteorology, GPS receivers and antennas are placed on satellites in Low Earth Orbit (LEO), and the signals transmitted by a GPS satellite are continuously recorded as a GPS satellite "rises" or "sets" behind the limb of the Earth. This process is called an occultation or a limb sounding. The GPS radio signals bend more as they encounter a thicker atmosphere and the bending (which causes an apparent increase in the length of the path of the radio signal) can be attributed to changes in temperature, pressure and water vapor along the path of the radio signal through the atmosphere that is nominally about 300 km long. The location of an occultation depends on the relative geometries of the GPS satellites in Mid Earth Orbit and the satellites in LEO. As a consequence, information about the vertical temperature, pressure and moisture structure of the Earth's atmosphere as a whole can be estimated with high accuracy, but not at any one particular place over time. The main difference between ground and space-based GPS meteorology is one of geometry. A space-based measurement can be thought of as a ground-based measurement turned on its side. For more information on space based GPS meteorology, the reader is referred to http://www.cosmic.ucar.edu/gpsmet/.

G.8. Montana Department of Transportation (MT DOT) Network

- Purpose of network: provide weather data to support management of Montana's transportation network.
- Primary management agency: MT DOT.
- Data website: http://www.met.utah.edu/jhorel/html/mesonet.
- Measured weather/climate elements:
  - Air temperature.
  - Relative humidity.
  - Wind speed and direction.
  - Wind gust and direction.

- Sampling frequency: unknown.
- Reporting frequency: unknown.
- Estimated station cost: unknown.
- Network strengths:
  o Real-time data.
  o Routine station maintenance.
- Network weaknesses:
  o Coverage is limited to the state of Montana.
  o Access to archived data can be difficult.

These weather stations are operated by MT DOT in support of management activities for Montana's transportation network. Measured meteorological elements include temperature, precipitation, wind, and relative humidity.

G.9. National Atmospheric Deposition Program (NADP)

- Purpose of network: measurement of precipitation chemistry and atmospheric deposition.
- Primary management agencies: USDA, but multiple collaborators.
- Data website: http://nadp.sws.uiuc.edu.
- Measured weather/climate elements:
  o Precipitation.
- Sampling frequency: daily.
- Reporting frequency: daily.
- Estimated station cost: unknown.
- Network strengths:
  o Data quality is excellent, with high data standards.
  o Site maintenance is excellent.
- Network weaknesses:
  o A very limited number of climate parameters are measured.

Stations within the NADP network monitor primarily wet deposition through precipitation chemistry at selected sites around the U.S. and its territories. The network is a collaborative effort among several agencies including USGS and USDA. Precipitation is the primary climate parameter measured at NADP sites. This network includes sites from the Mercury Deposition Network (MDN).

G.10. USDA/NRCS Snowcourse Network (NRCS-SC)

- Purpose of network: collect snowpack and related climate data to assist in forecasting water supply in the western U.S.
- Primary management agency: NRCS.
- Data website: http://www.wcc.nrcs.usda.gov/snowcourse/.
- Measured weather/climate elements:
  o Snow depth.
  o Snow water equivalent.
- Sampling, reporting frequency: monthly or seasonally.

- Estimated station cost: cost of man-hours needed to set up snowcourse and make measurements.
- Network strengths:
  o Periods of record are generally long.
  o Large number of high-altitude sites.
- Network weaknesses:
  o Measurement and reporting only occurs on monthly to seasonal basis.
  o Few weather/climate elements are measured.

USDA/NRCS maintains a network of snow-monitoring stations known as snowcourses. Many of these sites have been in operation since the early part of the twentieth century. These are all manual sites where only snow depth and snow water content are measured.

G.11. Remote Automated Weather Station (RAWS) Network

- Purpose of network: provide near-real-time (hourly or near hourly) measurements of meteorological variables for use in fire weather forecasts and climatology. Data from RAWS also are used for natural resource management, flood forecasting, natural hazard management, and air-quality monitoring.
- Primary management agency: WRCC, National Interagency Fire Center.
- Data website: http://www.raws.dri.edu/index.html.
- Measured weather/climate elements:
  o Air temperature.
  o Precipitation.
  o Relative humidity.
  o Wind speed.
  o Wind direction.
  o Wind gust.
  o Gust direction.
  o Solar radiation.
  o Soil moisture and temperature.
- Sampling frequency: 1 or 10 minutes, element-dependent.
- Reporting frequency: generally hourly. Some stations report every 15 or 30 minutes.
- Estimated station cost: $12000 with satellite telemetry ($8000 without satellite telemetry); maintenance costs are around $2000/year.
- Network strengths:
  o Metadata records are usually complete.
  o Sites are located in remote areas.
  o Sites are generally well-maintained.
  o Entire period of record available on-line.
- Network weaknesses:
  o RAWS network is focused largely on fire management needs (formerly focused only on fire needs).
  o Frozen precipitation is not measured reliably.
  o Station operation is not always continuous.
  o Data transmission is completed via one-way telemetry. Data are therefore recoverable

either in real-time or not at all.

The RAWS network is used by many land-management agencies, such as the BLM, NPS, Fish and Wildlife Service, Bureau of Indian Affairs, Forest Service, and other agencies. The RAWS network was one of the first automated weather station networks to be installed in the U.S. Most gauges do not have heaters, so hydrologic measurements are of little value when temperatures dip below freezing or reach freezing after frozen precipitation events. There are approximately 1100 real-time sites in this network and about 1800 historic sites (some are decommissioned or moved). The sites can transmit data all winter but may be in deep snow in some locations. The WRCC is the archive for this network and receives station data and metadata through a special connection to the National Interagency Fire Center in Boise, Idaho.

G.12. NWS/FAA Surface Airways Observation Network (SAO)

- Purpose of network: provide near-real-time (hourly or near hourly) measurements of meteorological variables and are used both for airport operations and weather forecasting.
- Primary management agency: NOAA, FAA.
- Data website: data are available from state climate offices, RCCs (e.g., WRCC, http://www.wrcc.dri.edu), and NCDC (http://www.ncdc.noaa.gov).
- Measured weather/climate elements:
  o Air temperature.
  o Dewpoint and/or relative humidity.
  o Wind speed.
  o Wind direction.
  o Wind gust.
  o Gust direction.
  o Barometric pressure.
  o Precipitation (not at many FAA sites).
  o Sky cover.
  o Ceiling (cloud height).
  o Visibility.
- Sampling frequency: element-dependent.
- Reporting frequency: element-dependent.
- Estimated station cost: $100000–$200000, with maintenance costs approximately $10000/year.
- Network strengths:
  o Records generally extend over several decades.
  o Consistent maintenance and station operations.
  o Data record is reasonably complete and usually high quality.
  o Hourly or sub-hourly data.
- Network weaknesses:
  o Nearly all sites are located at airports.
  o Data quality can be related to size of airport—smaller airports tend to have poorer datasets.
  o Influences from urbanization and other land-use changes.

These stations are managed by NOAA, U. S. Navy, U. S. Air Force, and FAA. These stations are located generally at major airports and military bases. The FAA stations often do not record precipitation, or they may provide precipitation records of reduced quality. Automated stations are typically ASOSs for the NWS or AWOSs for the FAA. Some sites only report episodically with observers paid per observation.

G.13. USDA/NRCS Soil Climate Analysis Network (SCAN)

- Purpose of network: comprehensive soil-climate network used in natural resource assessments and other conservation activities in the U.S.
- Primary management agency: USDA/NRCS.
- Data website: http://www.wcc.nrcs.usda.gov/scan/.
- Measured weather/climate elements:
  o Air temperature.
  o Precipitation.
  o Relative humidity.
  o Wind speed.
  o Wind direction.
  o Barometric pressure.
  o Solar radiation.
  o Snow water content.
  o Snow depth.
  o Soil moisture and temperature (enhanced sites only).
- Sampling frequency: 1-minute temperature; 1-hour precipitation, snow water content, and snow depth. Less than one minute for relative humidity, wind speed and direction, solar radiation, and soil moisture and temperature (all at enhanced site configurations only).
- Reporting frequency: reporting intervals are user-selectable. Commonly used intervals are every one, two, three, or six hours.
- Estimated station cost: $25000, with maintenance costs approximately $1000/year.
- Network strengths:
  o Sites are well-maintained.
  o Data are of high quality and are largely complete.
  o Very reliable automated system.
- Network weaknesses:
  o Short data records.
  o Network is still in development.

The SCAN network is intended to be a comprehensive nationwide soil moisture and climate information system to be used in supporting natural resource assessments and other conservation activities. These stations are usually located in the agricultural areas of the U.S. All SCAN sites are automated. The parameters measured at these sites include air temperature, precipitation, humidity, wind, barometric pressure, solar radiation, snow depth, and snow water content.

G.14. USDA/NRCS Snowfall Telemetry (SNOTEL) network

- Purpose of network: collect snowpack and related climate data to assist in forecasting water supply in the western U.S.

- Primary management agency: NRCS.
- Data website: http://www.wcc.nrcs.usda.gov/snow/.
- Measured weather/climate elements:
  o Air temperature.
  o Precipitation.
  o Snow water content.
  o Snow depth.
  o Relative humidity (enhanced sites only).
  o Wind speed (enhanced sites only).
  o Wind direction (enhanced sites only).
  o Solar radiation (enhanced sites only).
  o Soil moisture and temperature (enhanced sites only).
- Sampling frequency: 1-minute temperature; 1-hour precipitation, snow water content, and snow depth. Less than one minute for relative humidity, wind speed and direction, solar radiation, and soil moisture and temperature (all at enhanced site configurations only).
- Reporting frequency: reporting intervals are user-selectable. Commonly used intervals are every one, two, three, or six hours.
- Estimated station cost: $20000, with maintenance costs approximately $2000/year.
- Network strengths:
  o Sites are located in high-altitude areas that typically do not have other weather or climate stations.
  o Data are of high quality and are largely complete.
  o Very reliable automated system.
- Network weaknesses:
  o Historically limited number of elements.
  o Remote so data gaps can be long.
  o Metadata sparse and not high quality; site histories are lacking.
  o Measurement and reporting frequencies vary.
  o Many hundreds of mountain ranges still not sampled.
  o Earliest stations were installed in the late 1970s; temperatures have only been recorded since the 1980s.

USDA/NRCS maintains a set of automated snow-monitoring stations known as the SNOTEL (snowfall telemetry) network. These stations are designed specifically for cold and snowy locations. Precipitation and snow water content measurements are intended for hydrologic applications and water-supply forecasting, so these measurements are measured generally to within 2.5 mm (0.1 in.). Snow depth is tracked to the nearest 25 mm, or one inch. These stations function year around.

G.15. Union Pacific Railroad (UPR) Network

- Purpose of network: provide near-real-time meteorological data to support the shipping and transport activities of the Union Pacific Railroad.
- Primary management agency: Union Pacific Railroad.
- Data website: http://www.met.utah.edu/jhorel/html/mesonet.
- Measured weather/climate elements:

- o Air temperature.
- o Relative humidity.
- o Precipitation.
- o Wind speed and direction.
- o Wind gust and direction.
- Sampling frequency: unknown.
- Reporting frequency: unknown.
- Estimated station cost: unknown.
- Network strengths:
  - o Real-time data.
  - o Fairly extensive network (covers much of central and western U.S.).
- Network weaknesses:
  - o Uncertain data quality and station maintenance.
  - o Access to archived data is difficult.

This is a network of weather stations managed by UPR to support their shipping and transport activities, primarily in the central and western U.S. These stations are generally located along the UPR's main railroad lines. Measured meteorological elements include temperature, precipitation, wind, and relative humidity.

G.16. Weather For You Network (WX4U)

- Purpose of network: allow volunteer weather enthusiasts around the U.S. to observe and share weather data.
- Data website: http://www.met.utah.edu/jhorel/html/mesonet.
- Measured weather/climate elements:
  - o Air temperature.
  - o Relative humidity and dewpoint temperature.
  - o Precipitation.
  - o Wind speed and direction.
  - o Wind gust and direction.
  - o Barometric pressure.
- Sampling frequency: 10 minutes.
- Reporting frequency: 10 minutes.
- Estimated station cost: unknown.
- Network strengths:
  - o Stations are located throughout the U.S.
  - o Stations provide near-real-time observations.
- Network weaknesses:
  - o Instrumentation platforms can be variable.
  - o Data are sometimes of questionable quality.

The WX4U network is a nationwide collection of weather stations run by local observers. Meteorological elements that are measured usually include temperature, precipitation, wind, and humidity.

G.17. Wyoming Department of Transportation Network (WYDOT)

- Purpose of network: provide weather data to support management of Wyoming's transportation network.
- Primary management agency: WYDOT.
- Data website: http://www.met.utah.edu/jhorel/html/mesonet.
- Measured weather/climate elements:
  - Air temperature.
  - Relative humidity.
  - Pressure.
  - Wind speed and direction.
  - Wind gust and direction.
- Sampling frequency: unknown.
- Reporting frequency: unknown.
- Estimated station cost: unknown.
- Network strengths:
  - Real-time data.
  - Routine station maintenance.
- Network weaknesses:
  - Coverage is limited to the state of Wyoming.
  - Access to archived data can be difficult.

These weather stations are operated by WYDOT in support of management activities for Wyoming's transportation network. Measured meteorological elements include temperature, precipitation, wind, and relative humidity.

NPS/NGPN/NRTR—2007/039, May 2007

www.ingramcontent.com/pod-product-compliance
Lightning Source LLC
Chambersburg PA
CBHW081109290526
45795CB00006B/2064